JOSHUA
AND THE
CHILDREN

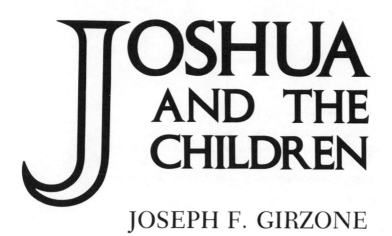

JOSHUA
AND THE
CHILDREN

JOSEPH F. GIRZONE

MACMILLAN PUBLISHING COMPANY

NEW YORK

Macmillan Publishing Company
866 Third Avenue, New York, N.Y. 10022
Collier Macmillan Canada, Inc.

Library of Congress-in-Publication Data
Girzone, Joseph F.
    Joshua and the children : a parable / Joseph F. Girzone.
        p.   cm.
    ISBN 0-02-543945-6
    I.   Title.
PS3557.I77J64   1989
813'.54—dc20   89-2615
                                                         CIP

10 9 8 7 6 5 4 3 2

Designed by Jack Meserole

Printed in the United States of America

In every age
There exist quiet heroes
Who, in their selfless devotion,
lay aside their own needs and comforts
and consecrate their energies and talents
to healing the wounds of a troubled humanity.
To these rare and often unhonored souls
this book is humbly dedicated.

ACKNOWLEDGMENTS

No creation is the work of one person. There are so many who have contributed in ways great and small to this work that it would be impossible to even identify them. I would, however, like to express my singular appreciation to Lorraine and Lester Bashant, my sister and her husband, and also their son, Joseph, for their unstinting and tireless efforts in assisting me during the difficult time preceding the creation of this manuscript.

JOSHUA
AND THE
CHILDREN

Quiet lay upon the meadow like a soft, green blanket. The sun, a globe of molten gold, shot laser beams across the fields and through the trees, burning away the early morning mist. The valley began springing to life. Rusty hinges of cottage doors squeaked open as farmers and factory workers slipped out into the narrow alleys to begin another day. The air was fresh and cool. A few friendly voices broke the stillness. A rooster crowed in the distance. A lone horse's hooves and wagon wheels clacked against the stone pavement. Peace reigned everywhere. If there were a heaven, its beauty and peace could not surpass the serenity of this countryside.

Michael Whitehead walked down the alley toward the main street on his way to work. "Good morning!" he yelled to his neighbor, Charlie Fellows.

"Good morning, Mike. It's too nice to work today. I'd rather be fishing."

Mike and Charlie had been friends since they were kids. They were inseparable. Mike was Catholic. Charlie was Presbyterian. It made no difference. Their families were close. Though they were not officially allowed to take part in each other's religious services, they were unofficially godfathers for each other's children. This did not sit too well with some individuals in town who wanted to keep everybody where they "belonged."

As the two men walked down the street together, a little voice called out, "Daddy, Daddy, you forgot your lunch again." It was Mike's daughter, Annie. She was only four and her father's pet. She and her brother, Pat, who was Charlie's godson, were running up the alley toward the main street, trying to catch up with their father.

As the two children reached the corner, barely a hundred feet behind the two men, an old beat-up car careened around the corner. A hand jerked open the window and tossed a grapefruit-sized object into the street just behind Mike and Charlie. It bounced and rolled away from the men and toward the children. The screeching tires were familiar sounds and almost always presaged some evil and violent act. The men reeled around, suspecting the worst. They saw the object and tried to warn the children, but it was too late. The thing exploded and hurled little Annie into the wall of the house on the corner, her father's lunch pail flying clear across the street. The boy, who was a few feet behind his sister, was somewhat shielded from the full impact of the explosion, but the force was so great, it lifted him off the ground and threw him to the stone pavement. His body was badly mangled.

Both men screamed in horror and disbelief. Instinctively, one man went to one child, the other to the other child. The girl was dead. The boy was in shock, unconscious, his left arm torn off and lying in the street a few feet away, his left leg cut in a hundred places and bleeding profusely. It would be a blessing if the child died. Mike cried like a baby, not knowing what to do with what remained of his son. Charlie told him Annie was dead and went to pick up the boy's arm. Mike made a tourniquet to control the bleeding from the stump, then picked up his son. Charlie carried the limp, lifeless body of the girl. The two men ran down the street as fast as they could to the doctor's house, praying that he would be home.

Joe Kelly, though everyone called him Tony, was a slow-moving, peaceful man. He talked little, but his quiet, thoughtful gaze missed nothing. One could tell he had seen a lot and felt deeply about everything but revealed nothing of what he thought. As early as it was, it was unusual to catch him home. He began his rounds of the village early each day, long before he went to the hospital.

Charlie knocked on the door. It opened immediately, as if someone had been waiting. It was the doctor. He winced when he saw the bleeding child in his father's arms. He told the men to put the children on the two examining tables in his office. He checked the girl. She was dead. He examined the boy and checked his vital signs. He was alive, but barely. Joe Kelly had a rare genius for diagnosis. He was careful and sure and usually right.

"We'll have to get him to the hospital immediately. Bring the arm here," he ordered as he readied a large plastic bag full of ice.

The three men went out the door to the doctor's jeep. Mike sat in the back seat with his son on his lap as the vehicle backed out into the street and started down the main street. There wasn't much traffic, so the doctor didn't use the siren, as he liked to do during busy hours, but used his CB radio to call the emergency ward at the hospital, telling the nurse what he wanted ready as soon as he got there. They would also need Dr. Stern, the microsurgeon. Although he worked in the big city, he lived nearby, and with any luck they could get him at home. There was no time to spare.

Everything went with perfect precision at the hospital. Dr. Kelly's cool manner kept everyone else calm. Dr. Stern arrived and said little, just examined the boy, the arm, consulted with another doctor, and went to work. The operation took a good part of the day. By late afternoon the arm was reattached, and the boy was resting in the recovery room.

While the doctors worked on Pat, Maureen, beside herself, came running into the hospital. She had been told by a neighbor some of what happened, but it was all garbled. She raced to the hospital and demanded to see her children. The nurses tried to calm her, but when she saw the dead body of her baby lying on the table, her face gray, she wailed like a person who had lost her mind.

It was the first tragedy to strike the young couple, and it came upon them with such devastating fury that it was impossible to control the emotion.

"Did you see who did it?" Maureen asked through her tears.

"No, they looked like strangers," Charlie said. Mike half agreed, but secretly was sure he recognized one of the men.

"They were after us," Charlie said. "But the kids were right behind us, and the grenade bounced in the street and rolled right toward them. They didn't have a chance. But we'll find out who did it."

That was little comfort to a mother whose daughter was dead and whose son's life was hanging by a thread. Mike put his arm around his wife, trying to comfort her. "I swear on my grandmother's grave I'll find who did it. I won't rest until I bring the cowards to justice, even if I have to do it myself," Mike said, not fully realizing what he said.

Charlie felt guilty for what happened. He knew it was because of his friendship with Mike that they did this. Their sick minds couldn't stand to see the love the two had for each other and for each other's families. He found it hard to face Maureen. However, being a true friend, he stayed with them right to the end.

The three of them remained at the hospital all day. Charlie called work and told the boss what had happened and said they wouldn't be in. There wasn't much they could do. Charlie said little, his just being there, just being a friend, was a comfort, though the thought that just being a friend was what brought all this on. It wouldn't have happened otherwise. Mike and Maureen thought the same thing, but banished the thought immediately. Charlie was too good a friend and loved the kids as much as if they were his own.

Late in the afternoon, Pat opened his eyes, looked at the three hovering over him, smiled faintly, and went back to sleep. The simple sign of recognition reassured them. The three stayed until evening and lights-out. If the child woke up, he would be given medication anyway. Besides, arrangements had to be made for Annie's funeral.

2

FUNERALS are commonplace in towns where religious wars are rampant. But each death is new to each family, and the devastation is always total. Little Annie's funeral was the more tragic because even the killers didn't mean to kill and maim these little kids. Fanatics like that have no guilt; they have long since numbed their twisted consciences so their blind self-righteousness translates cowardly murders into heroism. It was just a sad mistake that the kids got in the way. And so the murderers even went to the wake with a whitewashed conscience, without the slightest twinge of pity for the broken and distraught parents, who had done nothing to deserve this senseless tragedy.

The wake went far into the night. The whiskey flowed freely and the tongues flowed just as freely. Friends came from all over. Relatives like Jack and Mary Behan had come a long way, so they slept at the Whiteheads' cottage together with other relatives, who came from the four corners of the country, some from across the border. Charlie's pastor, Rev. Russell Davis, a Presbyterian minister, came to pay his respects. He was a decent man, and though quiet and seemingly shy, he was boldly outspoken in his condemnation of the senseless violence that was rampant throughout the county, thereby infuriating the agitators. People could always count on him to do the decent thing, like coming to little Annie's wake, which also galled his critics. When the Whiteheads' priest, Father Elmer Donnelly, came in, the two clergymen shook hands warmly, talked briefly, and then prayed the wake service together.

The next morning the church bells tolled heavy, somber tones as they called everyone to church, reminding young and old alike that life is serious business and death is no respecter of age or person. Charlie and his wife, Barbara, sat in the front pew with Mike and Maureen. It took no little amount of courage for them to do that, as they now had no delusions as to how much hatred and poison their friendship stirred up in sick minds. They were more determined than ever to stand by one another, even if every last one of the family was killed. Situations like this may breed violence, but they also breed a depth of heroism that is rare in the ordinary course of events.

Father Donnelly was an old man, a saintly man, who had consoled many a grief-stricken parent in his parish. He had been pastor there for over thirty years and knew everyone better than their own relatives. He had baptized them, heard their sins, given them Communion, married them, counseled them, comforted them, and eventually buried them. He was really the father of them all, and they felt that way about him. Some wished he would do more to end the senseless hatred and killing that went on; others thought he was already too outspoken and should mind his own business and stick to religion and stay out of politics, as if politics should be exempt from morals and none of God's business.

The sermon the priest gave was simple but poignant, with the kind of strong, tough comfort that would come from a man whose heart had been broken a thousand times and whose concern went much deeper than mere pious sentiment. "Mike and Maureen, and my dear friends . . . It is easy to say 'The Lord gives and the Lord takes,' and 'God takes only the good young,' but there are no words that can bring comfort to a mother and father whose child has died such a senseless death, and another is critically injured. My own heart breaks every time something like this happens, for I have grown old knowing all of you and loving all of you as if you were my very own. I share your grief and your sleepless nights, and your troubled concern for the future and for your children's future. For Annie the trouble is ended, the pain is no more. She is with God, walking happily with the Good Lord and His Blessed Mother. The pain of her leaving is our pain. She is at peace and happy and safe in God's home. I used to be afraid to die. Lately, as the pain all around us grows ever worse, the prospects of seeing God do not appear so frightening, offering, as they do, the hope of liberation from the agony of living in this troubled world.

"However, we still live in this world, and our work is not finished. In the face of this senseless tragedy, we have arrived at a critical juncture in our lives. We can allow ourselves to live in hatred like those who killed little Annie, and add to the endless hatred we see all around us, or follow Our Savior as Christians and be like Him, who never allowed himself to take offense but forgave even those who plotted to destroy him, like they still do in our own day. 'Whatever you do to the least of my brothers and sisters, you do to me.' And in Annie's death, they killed Christ once again."

As the priest said those words he was distracted by two men in the congregation whose faces became distorted

with a look that seethed with anger and guilt. And he
knew that they were the ones who had killed the little girl.
They were not total strangers. He had seen them around
but did not know who they were or where they were from.
He didn't remember them as children growing up in the
town. They must be recent imports from someplace else.

Regaining his composure, the priest continued, "It is
at times like this that it is not easy to be a Christian, and
that is what should separate us from the rest of the world.
'An eye for an eye and a tooth for a tooth' may make sense
to a heart that is filled with grief and to a feverish mind
that can find no relief even in sleep, but forgiveness is the
beautiful gift that Jesus gave us as the unfailing key to
peace of mind.

"Over a hundred years ago in France, a butler attached
to a wealthy family knew where the family kept all their
wealth, hidden in a vault underneath the château. He
methodically plotted to kill everyone in the family and steal
the treasure. One night, when everyone was asleep, he
murdered first the father and mother, and then, one by
one, the children. Only the youngest escaped because he
had heard noises and couldn't sleep. When he realized
what was happening he quietly slipped out of his room and
hid in a closet under a pile of clothes.

"For years he wandered the streets as an orphan, and
later entered the seminary and became a priest. Eventually
he was assigned to Devil's Island as a chaplain. One
afternoon a convict came running in from the fields,
frantically calling for the chaplain. 'There's a man dying
out in the field, Father, come quickly.'

"The priest ran out with him and reached the dying
man. Kneeling down beside him, he lifted his head onto
his lap and asked if he would like to confess his sins. The

dying man refused. 'Why, my son?' the priest asked. 'Because God will never forgive me for what I have done.'

" 'But what have you done that is so bad?' the priest continued. And the man went on to tell the story of how he had killed this whole family so he could have their money, and only the little boy escaped because he couldn't find him.

"Then the priest said to him, 'If I can forgive you, certainly God can forgive you. And I forgive you from my heart. It was my family you killed, and I am that little boy.'

"The convict cried and told the priest how he had been haunted all his life over what he had done, though no one else knew about it. Even the authorities never found out.

"The two men cried together. And, as the priest was giving the dying man absolution, the man died with his head resting on the priest's lap.

"My children," Father Donnelly continued, "that story is a true story, and has been the inspiration of my life whenever people have hurt me. It shows how beautiful and godly is the kind of forgiveness that Jesus taught. Trying to forgive like that has brought me much peace during my life, and I share that story with you in the hope that you may be able to follow in Jesus' footsteps and forgive those evil men who have done this horrible thing to your children, and find peace in your own souls. May the Good Lord fill your hearts with his peace and grant your other children a happy and peaceful life."

The priest continued the Mass, watching every now and then the two men he had identified during the sermon. They knew he was watching and lowered their eyes whenever he looked their way.

The Mass ended. The procession to the cemetery and

the committal service was without incident. Mike and Maureen clung to each other during the prayers, and when it was over, thanked Father Donnelly for his comfort and support and asked him over to the house for refreshments with the family.

CHAPTER 3

THE VILLAGE SQUARE was quiet in the early morning. Men had gone to work, women were at home doing their chores. Children were still not used to summer vacation. The sun was shining through the trees, lighting up the square with a fresh, warm glow. The mist that hung over the meadow at dawn had been burned away by the sun, but you could still smell manure and the fragrance of wet grass.

Three roads met at the square: Stonecastle Road, which came down the hill from the north; Downers Road, which came in from the east and snaked its way through the village, and Maple Street, which came in through the fields from the south. The square itself was small, about three times the size of a basketball court, but was the center of whatever activity took place in the town. At one time the square had been set with cobblestones, but lately these had been coated with cement—none too professionally, as the rounded tops of the stones were still evident. Lining the north side of the square was a row of buildings that had probably been built before the turn of the century, well over a hundred years ago. Most of them were brick. There was a general store, a meat market, a small apothecary shop, and, at the end of the row, a little tavern from which could be heard laughter and boisterous sounds at almost any time during the day or night. Hanging in front of the establishment was a faded wooden sign bearing the name "Almost Home," which the place was for many of its frequenters, though some never quite made it to their homes.

Across from the row of brick buildings, on the opposite side of the square, stretched a vast meadow where sheep and cattle and goats grazed lazily all during the day. A row of ancient maple trees separated the meadow from the square, and in front of the trees there was a stone wall that went the distance of the square. Other buildings lining the main street and what few side streets there were formed the village proper. Most of the people lived in cottages scattered on roads winding their way through the meadows.

There were four churches in town: Presbyterian, Roman Catholic, Anglican, and Wesleyan. The Presbyterian church was by far the largest, having most of the people in town as its congregation. It was located just north of the village on the hillside, and was impressive with its tall, pointed steeple overlooking the village and the surrounding countryside. The Catholic church was a small brick building located at the southern end of town and bordering on the meadow. It was more a chapel than a church. It was quaint and resembled an oversized cottage rather than a church building. Climbing roses clung to the front and sides of the building. At the one side of the church was the churchyard, lined with gravestones set in precise rows. On the other side was another yard used for parish socials. The Anglican church was a stately building constructed of imported stone, with dignified stained-glass windows. A bell tower stood next to the church. Its six bells, which were the pride of the parish, were exposed to view and could be heard at the far ends of the meadow. Surrounding the tower was a carefully manicured garden. The Wesleyan church was a small Tudor-style building just down the street from the Catholic church. It was surrounded by a white picket fence, with flowering shrubs placed discreetly at intervals both inside and outside the fence.

It was about ten o'clock. The waking village was still tranquil. The only sounds were the whistling of cardinals in a nearby bush, and the cawing of crows high up in a maple tree, and a child's voice calling a playmate. A lonely figure was walking toward the square from Stonecastle Road. He was wearing khaki pants, with a brown pullover shirt and sandals. He was of medium height, slim, with attractive features and wavy chestnut hair. His walk suggested a free spirit who seemed to have not a care in the world.

He entered the square and walked over to a bench near the stone wall that ran along the south end of the square. He sat down, took a handkerchief from his pocket and wiped his brow, then surveyed the scene as if planning a strategy. The village was just beginning to come alive. There were kids on bicycles delivering packages, other younger children coming from here and there, calling their friends to come and play with them. A girl who couldn't have been more than six years old came walking into the square carrying a bag of what must have been seeds or peanuts, and she was immediately deluged by an army of pigeons and birds of every description. They were obviously expecting her. She walked along the wall, throwing out small handfuls of food as she went, gradually approaching the bench where the stranger was sitting.

As she approached the stranger said hello to her, calling her by name. The girl was surprised.

"How do you know my name?" she asked.

"I have known you all your life, Jane. I can see you have a lot of friends."

"Yes, I feed them every day. Would you like some seeds to feed the birds?" the little girl asked the friendly stranger. She was surprisingly unafraid, although she had never seen the man before.

"Yes, I would like that very much." The man held his hand out as the girl poured some of the seeds into it. Immediately a pigeon landed on the man's hand and began to eat. Other birds flew over, but were not as bold as the pigeon. They landed on the ground and waited impatiently. The girl threw some seeds to them and they demolished them in an instant.

"What's your name, sir?" the little girl asked the stranger.

"Joshua," the man replied.

"Do you live around here? I've never seen you before."

"I just came into town. I'll be here for a while."

"Do you know how old I am?" Jane asked, then answered before Joshua had time to say a word. "I'm six years old, and I come out here every morning to feed the birds. Some of them come and eat out of my hand. I love those redbirds that hide in the bushes, but they won't come near me. See, there's one now." The girl pointed to a cardinal perched on a large maple branch hanging over the bench.

"That bird is called a cardinal," the stranger said, then asked, "Would you like him to come to you?"

"I'd love him to, but he never does."

The stranger looked up at the bird nervously dancing on the branch. He held out his hand with a few seeds in it and called the bird. The bird looked for a second, then flew over to the man's hand.

"Now, take some seeds in your hand and very slowly put your hand out," Joshua instructed the girl.

As she did so Joshua moved his hand ever so gently toward the girl's hand. When the bird finished the seeds in Joshua's hand, he paused, looked at the girl, then at Joshua, then made a timid move over to the girl's hand. Little Jane was thrilled. The bird finished the seeds and flew back up into the tree.

Jane was delighted. She loved those little redbirds, but they were always so nervous, they would never go near anyone. She never dreamed she would ever hold one in her hand.

"Thank you, Joshua," Jane said to the stranger, then asked him how he learned to do that.

"Oh, I guess the birds aren't afraid of me," he answered simply.

"But he came to you as soon as you called him," the girl persisted.

"Perhaps he recognized my voice," Joshua replied. That seemed to satisfy the girl.

"You are a nice man, Joshua," Jane said. "Would you stay here until I go and tell my friends about you? I would like them to meet you."

"Yes. I would like to meet your friends," Joshua responded.

In no time at all Jane returned with her friends, mostly girls, but also a few boys. Joshua was sitting on the bench, watching people as they went about their work. An old man smoking a pipe had just left him. The children said hello to him as they walked past him and approached the bench.

"Joshua, these are my friends," Jane said. "This is Mary, and Joan, and Nancy, and Patricia, and Eleanor, and Frances, and Meredith. And these are friends too," she said as she pointed out the boys. "This is Tom, and Mike, and Edmund, and Joe."

"I am very happy to meet all of you. It looks like you all are good friends. Joe, do you play that trumpet you are carrying?" Joshua asked.

"Yes," the little boy answered shyly.

"Would you show me how to play it?" Joshua asked him.

The boy was embarrassed to show off in front of his friends, but, seeing it meant so much to the stranger, he obliged.

Joshua watched intently. The boy played a few simple notes and asked Joshua if he wanted to try.

"Yes, I would."

Joe gave Joshua the instrument and watched the man put it to his lips. He blew into it once, then again, and again. Finally a note emerged, rather weak and sickly, but a note all the same. He tried again. A dismal, low-sounding grunt, like a sick cow. The children tried not to laugh. But Joshua wouldn't give up. He concentrated and tried again. This time notes came out firm and clear. He continued to experiment and after a minute or so was able to play something that sounded reasonably pleasant.

The boy offered to show him how to play other notes and a simple melody. Joshua watched and then tried again. This time he did better. The children all clapped and cried out, "Hurray! Hurray! Joshua can play the trumpet."

"Joshua," Joe asked as the man returned the trumpet, "do you live near here? We've never seen you before."

"Not far," Joshua said simply.

"Why are you here in our village?" Mary asked.

"I heard you are nice people here and I wanted to come and visit."

"Where will you stay?" she persisted.

"Wherever. I'm not concerned. The weather is nice and it is cool at night on the hill in the meadow. I can stay in that grove of trees up there," Joshua said as he pointed to the trees in the distance.

The children were amused at the casual unconcern of the man. But they had seen other strangers with no apparent roots wandering through their village, so they were not surprised.

"Will you be here in the square tomorrow?" Jane asked Joshua.

"Yes."

"Oh, good! I will bring my brother and his friends down to meet you," the girl added excitedly. "You'll like my brother. His name is Matt and he plays a guitar."

"I'm sure I will like him," Joshua responded.

The children said good-bye and promised to come back the next morning. They ran off, talking excitedly about their newfound friend. Simple little things were thrilling to these children who had few material things and managed to create their own fun and enjoyment out of each new event in their life.

CHAPTER 4

WHEN Jane went home and told her mother about Joshua, her mother was upset that her daughter would be so forward with a stranger.

"But, Mommy," the girl protested, "it's not as if he's a stranger. He's so gentle. I felt he was my friend right away. There's nothing to be afraid of. Joey even taught him how to play his trumpet. And when he made funny notes and we laughed, he laughed too. He's really different. He's not like anybody I've met before. Come and see for yourself. He'll be in the square tomorrow."

All day the girl kept telling her friends about this man she had met in the square who called to the redbird in the tree and it came to him, and he let her hold the bird in her hand. "You have to come and meet him," she told everybody.

Joe went home and told his teenage brother Paul about Joshua and insisted he should come and meet him. Paul wasn't impressed, but to appease his brother, promised to come and meet the man the next day.

Later in the afternoon stories circulated around the village about an incident in the nearby city. It seemed a jeep filled with soldiers was patrolling a trouble-ridden neighborhood when someone threw a Molotov cocktail at the jeep and killed one of the soldiers. According to rumor, it was a teenager who threw the thing, but the soldiers, who were too occupied trying to save their burning companion, let the youth escape.

Whenever these incidents occurred everyone paid the price. The atmosphere became tense and people were jittery, watching for the slightest sign of trouble. Parents tried to keep their children off the streets and as near to home as possible. Added patrols rolled through the village as a warning to potential troublemakers.

Around suppertime a handful of not-too-steady individuals filed out of the tavern and wandered off in all directions on their way home. One of the men had to cross the field opposite the square. He was a ruddy-faced young fellow named Tim, who had a pointed face and a sharp, pointed nose and broad, thin lips. He was tall, and his long legs moved in almost disjointed steps, giving him an air of carefreeness, which was even more heightened by the double shots he had just had at the tavern. Whistling a tune as he ambled across the field, he was caught short as he passed the ancient oak that stood majestically in the middle of the field.

A figure was sitting under the tree eating what was apparently his supper. As Tim passed he waved a casual hello to the man and was caught short when the stranger responded by calling him by his name, "Good evening, Tim. It's a fine, cool breeze tonight."

Tim was shocked. "How'd you know my name? Who are you? I've never seen you around before."

"My name is Joshua. I'm just sitting here eating my supper. Would you like some?"

"No, thanks. How'd you know my name?"

"I could just tell when I looked at you," Joshua answered simply.

Tim was too curious not to stop and engage the man in some small talk. "What are you eating?" Tim asked.

"Some fish I just caught in the stream. Here, have a piece," Joshua said as he took a moist chunk from the little fire and held it out to the tall, skinny figure hovering over him.

Tim awkwardly and rather reluctantly accepted and ate it.

"Never ate fish like this before. Not bad. In fact, it's better than the way my wife cooks it," Tim said with a broad smile, then sat down on a log lying nearby.

"You look like too refined a man to be just wandering around shiftless. What do you do for a living?" Tim asked good-naturedly.

"Right now I'm sort of vacationing," Joshua answered simply. "I like people, and I enjoy visiting new places and meeting new people. You have a friendly town here, and I like your people."

"You might not have liked it if you had seen what happened the other day. Two little kids were blown up by some nuts driving through town. They intended to kill the kids' father and a friend for being friends. One is a Protestant, the other is a Catholic. They've been friends since childhood, and everyone thought it was beautiful that they stayed friends even when they grew up, everyone, that is, except a few nuts."

"That's sad. But I still think your people are nice people," Joshua insisted.

"Aren't you worried, traveling around so freely, that you might get caught up in some kind of police net or be suspect by one side or the other?" Tim asked, fishing to see where Joshua stood on these matters.

"No, that doesn't bother me. I don't concern myself

with politics. They create artificial categories that are unreal, and divide people, and prevent people from thinking and living the way they want. Freedom is sacred."

As the two men were finishing their food, Tim asked Joshua where he intended to sleep for the night. Joshua said he would probably sleep in the field under the tree. Tim thought that unnecessary and invited him to stay at his house. Joshua accepted. The two men walked off together.

CHAPTER 5

It was not far to Tim's house, just across the meadow. Everyone was waiting impatiently for the head of the house to come home so they could eat supper. It had become accepted routine for Tim to come home late, not because the family approved, but because no one could do anything about it. Tim's shaky appearance didn't enhance his coming, and his bringing a total unknown with him added to the annoyance.

"Stella," Tim said to his wife, with a sheepish look on his face, "this is my new friend. I found him eating by himself in the meadow. His name is Joshua. He's a good man and doesn't have much use for politics, so everyone can relax. He's already eaten supper, but he might like something to drink." With that Tim went to the refrigerator and took out a beer and gave it to his friend.

Everyone eyed Joshua, not knowing what to make of him. He looked embarrassed, sensing the tension in the house. Stella felt his uneasiness, and being a kind person, she welcomed him with a cheerful smile and introduced him to all the family. There were four children in the McGirr family, two boys and two girls. Tim's mother also lived with them in the crowded bungalow.

The house was small. There was just a large kitchen that opened into a living room—really just one room divided by the difference in furniture—and three small bedrooms, one where Tim and Stella slept and the other two where the children slept. There wasn't much privacy. The grandmother slept in a bed against the wall in the living room. It was closer to the bathroom and more convenient for her. On nights when she couldn't sleep, she could slip out on the front porch and rock herself to sleep in the rocking chair.

Introductions over, the family sat down to eat. Everyone waited for Tim to say grace, which he usually forgot. This night was usual. He started to eat, saw that everyone else had their hands folded waiting for grace, then half choked on his first bite, which he didn't know whether to take out of his mouth or swallow.

"In the name of the Father and of the Son and of the Holy Ghost. Amen. Dear Lord," Tim prayed, "we thank you for the food we eat this evening and for my dear wife, who works so hard to prepare it, and for the children and for mother, who blesses us with her presence. We also thank you for our new friend, Joshua. May his presence bless our home. Bless us all with good health and grant peace to our land. We ask this in Jesus' name." Everyone responded with a hearty "Amen" and immediately attacked the food.

Conversation at the table was subdued because of the inhibiting presence of a stranger. Everyone was curious about Joshua. Who was he? Where was he from? Did he work? What was he doing in their village? Joshua answered simply and before long even the children were fascinated by his rare talent for conversation as he told of his experiences in the different places he visited recently and what the people were like in those places.

Tim tried to feel out Joshua about his feelings on the

situation between the Protestants and the Catholics. Joshua's answer was simple: God's children have to learn to love one another. He wants his children to be one. Barriers are artificial. They make people believe they are different. God doesn't create barriers. People do. Beneath the surface there is little difference between those on either side. Once they stop hating, they will wonder why they were even fighting.

"My friend," Tim said, "I'm afraid you make it too simple. It's been going on for a long time."

"Time doesn't consecrate it," Joshua replied calmly, "nor does it justify what is happening. The causes were different centuries ago, and the issues today are not the same. They can be worked out by reasonable people. Fear and hatred should give way to understanding. The real damage today is to little children. They have a right to live and to grow up free of hatred. Parents who teach their children to hate destroy their own children and condemn them to go through life with tortured souls and twisted minds, never knowing peace in their hearts, the peace that Jesus wanted so much to give."

Tim and Stella had managed to keep aloof from the embroilments of the town and the city nearby. The kids worked their little farm during the school year and all summer. Milking the cows and goats, feeding the chickens and ducks, and tending the crops kept them busy and away from activities in the town and from other children. Their parents taught them early in their lives to avoid trouble-makers and children who hang around in gangs. This served them well, as they were able to grow up free from the troubled feelings of so many of the children of their time. They were happy children, and it showed in the spontaneous way they laughed and reacted to life.

While everyone was finishing supper the two girls quietly cleared the table, and Stella filled a teakettle and put it on to boil, then cut up freshly baked soda bread and placed it on the table. Joshua had never tasted soda bread before and was eager to try it. Tim thought it would be a good idea to have the tea and bread on the porch since it was such a cool evening. Everyone agreed, so they retired outside. The soda bread was a treat. Even Joshua thought so and readily accepted a second piece when it was offered.

Tim's mother, Anne, was a pleasant woman in her late sixties who had a fine wit. She kept eyeing Joshua all during the evening, and when she finally thought she had him sized up, she opened up with her first remark. "Joshua, you're a fine-looking man, if I might say so, and too good a man to be living in this tough world. You look too refined to cope with what's going on these days. I hope no evil befalls you."

"Thank you, Anne," Joshua replied kindly. "I've experienced a lot and understand human beings quite well. They don't frighten me. My life is carefully planned by my Father, and no one approaches without his willing it. So I'm never afraid." It was a rather odd kind of response, which made everyone wonder, but no one felt comfortable enough to ask him to clarify.

As the sun set, directly across from the front porch, a beautiful golden glow spread all along the horizon. Swallows and nightingales could be seen silhouetted against the golden light as they glided gracefully across the vast ocean of cool evening air.

Stella offered to give up Tim's and her bedroom for the evening, but Joshua wouldn't hear of it. He was used to sleeping outdoors and asked if they minded his sleeping in the hammock on the front porch. He had never slept in anything like that before and thought it would be fun.

It wasn't long before they all retired. But before finally turning in, Stella peeked through the curtain to see if Joshua was comfortable in the hammock. He wasn't there. She looked around the porch and in the moonlight spotted him on his knees in the grass, sitting on his heels, with arms extended, deep in prayer. He looked so beautiful. She wondered who he really was.

CHAPTER

Joshua was the first one up
the next morning, with the singing birds and the first rays
of dawn. The air was fresh and clean. Joshua breathed in
the clear, cool air in deep drafts, savoring each breath as it
filled his lungs. A cock crowed. It reminded him of Peter
long ago. What a sad night that was! It seemed like such a
short time ago. Cows were mooing in the barn, calling the
children to relieve them of their heavy burden of swollen
udders.

Joshua walked about the farmyard, noticing everything. The animals fascinated him. The fields were
carefully tended and showed how well disciplined the
children were in following their father's instructions. It
was mostly their job, as their father worked in an automo-
bile factory in the city and had no mind for farming when
he came home. He had worked the farm for years before he
got his job at the factory, and had trained the kids to work
with him since they were little children. They always
enjoyed it, and now that they were older, and did practically all the work, they were allowed to keep for their
savings accounts a good part of what they earned from the
farm.

At the side of the barn was a fenced-off section where
the sheep rested overnight. It was safer that way as there

were still foxes roaming the hills and meadow. Joshua walked past the sheep. There was something about the sheep that always struck a sentimental chord in Joshua. He leaned on the fence and watched them, the little ones with funny, shaky legs, keeping close to their mothers, looking back nervously over their shoulders, watching Joshua.

"Joshua, Joshua," a voice called out through the early morning silence, "are you still here?"

Joshua turned around and saw the youngest of the family, Christopher, on the front porch, an arm wrapped around a porch post, looking up and down the yard for him. Chris had a whimsical little face and a heavy crop of brown curly hair. He hadn't said a word all evening, just kept watching Joshua, absorbing everything about him, finally deciding he liked him. When he woke up Joshua was the first thing on his mind. He hoped he hadn't disappeared during the night. As soon as he dressed he ran out on the porch to find him.

"Here I am," Joshua called back, "down near the sheep pen."

Chris got tongue-tied all of a sudden and didn't know what to say. He just stood there, happy his friend hadn't gone.

Joshua walked up to the house. As he approached Chris froze, not knowing what to do but smile, which said everything he wanted to say in words but couldn't. He did get up enough nerve to tell Joshua that breakfast was ready. They went inside together.

Tim was all ready for work and was standing in the corner sipping a mug of steaming black coffee. Stella was frying eggs and ham. The children had brought the eggs in fresh from the yard while biscuits were baking in the oven.

Grandma had just finished saying her rosary. Those prayers to the Mother of God had been her strength during the hard years after her husband had been killed by a Protestant fanatic almost fifteen years ago. In spite of it she managed to raise her children remarkably free from hatred and bigotry.

"Good morning, Joshua," Tim greeted his guest as Christopher ushered him quietly into the kitchen and sat him down at the table next to his place. At that point the other children, Pat and Tom and Ann, burst through the front door. They had just finished their chores at the barn. Everyone took his place, and Tim asked Joshua if he would say grace. He consented.

Taking a biscuit from the bread basket, he broke it in half, closed his eyes, and prayed, "Father, bless this family with your love and protection. Keep them from harm and let no evil touch them, for they preserve your love and forgiveness in a troubled land. Bless this food to nourish their bodies, and may your word nourish their souls as we cannot live on bread alone. Fill their lives with your joy and peace." Everyone responded with a thoughtful "Amen."

Joshua passed the two halves of the biscuit to those on his right and left and told each one to take a piece. Christopher was thrilled. He took a piece and passed it on.

"What a beautiful custom!" Grandma McGirr commented. "Where did you learn that, Joshua?"

"It was a custom in my family, and I added a new symbolism to it, to give it more meaning," he answered simply.

The McGirrs were happy people. Though they had suffered immensely from the bitter hatreds all around them, they remained free of spite and vengeance and exuded a carefree joy and lightheartedness that was infectious. It showed in a powerful way that another person's hatred does not have to fill the victim's life with hate unless he freely chooses to hate. The meanness of another merely provides an excuse to hate, but never a valid reason.

Because the McGirrs were happy people, mealtime was fun, even if Tim did come in late. Grandma was never pompous. As old as she was, and she was approaching seventy, she could still tell an old joke she remembered from years ago or poke fun gently at one of the children. They would go along with it and laugh. Joshua himself seemed pleased with this beautiful family.

Tim finished breakfast first and readied himself for work as Joshua, ready to leave with Tim, was finishing up. Everyone seemed sad at the thought of Joshua leaving. It was strange. They had only met him the night before, but there was something about this simple, gentle man that captured their hearts and they didn't want to lose what they found in him.

As Tim and Joshua walked out the door, Stella kissed Tim shyly and to Joshua extended her hand, which he shook warmly. The children stood by silently. Christopher had a tear in his eye but bravely held it back. Joshua thanked them all for their kind hospitality and rested his hand on Christopher's head as if in blessing. The two men started down the path toward the meadow. Everyone felt sad and wondered if Joshua would come to visit them again.

No sooner had Joshua appeared in the village square than children started flocking around him, their curiosity aroused by the stories spread about him overnight. Even some of the older kids, curious and casual, hung around the square, talking in small cliques, feigning total disinterest in the little children's newfound hero.

Joe came back with his trumpet to show off a new tune he had been practicing all night. He couldn't wait to give Joshua another lesson. Another boy, Andrew, brought a guitar and waited patiently for his turn to show his skills.

"Joshua," Joe asked a bit shyly, "would you like to play my trumpet again?"

"Yes, maybe I can do a little better today," Joshua replied with a grin. Taking the shiny silver instrument, he put it to his lips and tried to play. Only a few sour notes belched forth. He tried again, and as his lips adjusted to the mouthpiece, the notes came clear and sharp. He played the tune Joe had taught him the day before, and then played a tune he had just made up, a happy tune with funny notes that made everyone laugh. Even Joe was amazed at how fast Joshua learned. He offered to give Joshua another lesson. Joshua agreed, and the child taught this grown-up stranger how to play other notes and another simple tune. The kids were surprised at the humility of this adult who would let a child teach him and thoroughly enjoyed learning from him.

Joshua had been noticing Andrew's patience while he waited for his turn with Joshua. "Andrew," Joshua called to him, "you are a patient little lad. Come here and let me see your guitar. Do you play it well?"

Andrew was beside himself with pride. "Yes, I think I do. Would you like to hear me play it?"

"I'd love to," Joshua responded with interest. The boy started to strum his guitar, and before long was lost in his music. The boy was good. He played a folk song, and the other children at first started humming, then began to sing. Before long they were all singing, even Joshua, once he picked up the melody.

It wasn't by chance that all the children gathering around Joshua were Catholic. Jane, the little girl who fed the birds, was Catholic, so her friends would naturally be Catholic. But it wasn't just her friends who came. There were others who had heard about this strange fellow wandering around. Any new activity was bound to arouse interest, the town being small and the amusements limited.

As Joshua was watching Andrew, so absorbed in his music, he noticed another group of children walking into the square. They looked no different from the children around Joshua, but they remained aloof and stayed off by themselves near the inn at the opposite side of the square. There were about ten of them and they were about the same age as the children with Joshua, which was on average twelve to fourteen years. In spite of their obvious curiosity, none of the children approached Joshua's group. They stood there, just watching, with a detectable look of envy at the fun Joshua's friends were having.

The group of older children, who had originally come to the square and kept to themselves, had gradually moved closer to Joshua's group and were now part of the chorus singing along to Andrew's accompaniment. Even though they were with younger kids, they had forgotten themselves and were really having fun.

The children must have been with Joshua the good part of an hour, then began to drift off in different directions until Joshua was left alone in the square. Resting on the stone wall, he looked up and down the square as if in deep thought, with no trace of the childlike playfulness of a few minutes before, but more like a military officer planning strategy for an upcoming encounter.

Then, with a determined look, he walked across the square and down the street, past a row of houses and shops, took a right turn at the last street in the town, and headed for the Catholic church. It looked pretty with all the roses in bloom. A man who appeared to be in his early seventies was on his knees working in the garden. Hearing footsteps approaching, he looked up and saw Joshua.

"Hello, young man," he said in a friendly voice. "Coming for a visit?"

"Yes, I thought I'd stop by. My name is Joshua," he answered.

"Are you new in town?"

"Yes," Joshua replied. "I've been traveling around the country and noticed what a quaint, friendly village you have, so I decided to stay awhile."

"I'm Father Donnelly," the old man said as he got up

off his knees none too easily. Joshua stretched out a hand, offering to help him, but the old man made it on his own.

The two men shook hands, and the priest welcomed Joshua into his garden and automatically started showing him around.

"What a beautiful garden you have!" Joshua commented.

"Thank you," the priest responded, with a gleam of pride in his eyes. "Yes, I've been cultivating this garden for over thirty years now; it's like a little piece of heaven for me. I know I should be able to find God in the church, but for some reason I feel closer to him out here in the garden, so I spend most of my time here lately. It takes my mind off all the hurt around our neighborhood." A tear appeared in the old man's eyes. Joshua noticed and understood.

The priest had been there a long time. He was a member of every family, yet, belonging to none, he was very much alone. It was difficult getting too intimate with the people. A priest couldn't pick friends without others feeling left out, so he stayed pretty much to himself. God was his only real friend. Joshua knew that, so he came to visit.

Up to that point the old man, being distracted by his garden, hadn't looked directly at Joshua, but as he stood there talking to him he turned and looked into Joshua's eyes. He was immediately taken aback by what he saw in them—a look of intense compassion—and he had the strangest feeling this stranger could see into his very soul. The old priest's first impulse was to look away, out of embarrassment, but when he saw nothing critical in the man's eyes, he continued to stare.

After showing Joshua around the garden, the priest invited him into the church. It was a typical, old-fashioned country church, with rough-hewn wooden beams and rafters and almost life-size statues, which seemed to come to life as the red and blue and yellow lights from the stained-glass windows played tricks on the faces of the saints. The priest told Joshua he had bought the statues long ago with his own money. They were gifts to the people, simple reminders of the closeness of their sainted friends, telling them that they should be used as aids to prayer and to focus their minds on the things of the spirit, but never as objects of devotion in themselves, like a picture of a mother or a departed loved one.

Joshua was impressed with the simplicity of the church and told the priest he would like to spend a few minutes talking to God. The priest understood and said he would be working in the garden when he finished.

Joshua knelt and prayed. He was a beautiful sight, kneeling erect, with strong, delicate hands loosely folded, and his face relaxed and calm. You could sense the total absorption of his thoughts in a world to which no one else had access.

After a few minutes Joshua finished and walked back out into the garden. The priest was waiting, wiping his brow with a blue handkerchief. Standing there in his soiled black pants and wrinkled, faded white shirt, the old man looked more like the hired hand than the parish priest. He was glad the stranger had come along. He had distracted him from his troubled thoughts, thoughts over his own fast-approaching twilight and the events of recent days, which presaged no good for the future.

"Young man," the priest said, "would you like to have a cup of tea with me and a little snack? It's almost time for me to take a rest. I can't work long like I used to."

"Yes, I'd like that," Joshua answered cheerfully. The

two men went into the parish house. The housekeeper, Marie MacCarthy, opened the door when she heard the footsteps approaching. As she welcomed Joshua, the priest introduced her, telling Joshua what a help she was, since he was getting too old to prepare his own meals, and he said, "She is a real angel of mercy to many in the parish. She even helps Protestants." Everyone chuckled.

The two men sat down.

"You've been here a long time, Father, haven't you?" Joshua remarked as he scanned the kitchen and noticed all the accumulated mementos hanging here and there around the room.

"Yes, sometimes I think too long," the old man answered rather wistfully.

"Why do you say that?" Joshua asked, concerned,

"Because there is so much hurt and anguish to life," the priest responded. "The burden on the heart gets heavier as you get older. Parents and family die, loved ones leave, children whom you have known from infancy grow up and come to pour their hearts out over their problems. And there are no little problems in our modern world. The problems today only God can solve. They are much too big for the human mind to even grasp, much less attempt to resolve. I go to bed every night with a heavy heart. I ache for each one in my parish; they have become more dear to me than my own family. The hurt is sometimes too much to bear." It all poured out as if the old man had been waiting for Joshua to come along. He could not talk to anyone in his parish this way. Indeed, who could he talk to like this who would ever understand? The tea ready, Marie poured a cup for each of them and put a newly baked loaf of soda bread on the table. The priest cut off a few slices and pushed the plate in front of Joshua.

"That is what makes you a good shepherd," Joshua said, trying to comfort him, fully intending all that the remark implied. The priest looked at him, wondering again about this stranger who seemed to know him so thoroughly, though they had just met.

Surprised, the priest asked him, "How do you know me?"

"Before you were born I knew you."

"But you are barely forty years old. How could you have known me?"

"Everyone knows in his own way. I have known you and have watched your work. You have labored hard and long for my Father's sheep, and you are dear to God. Don't be afraid."

"But I am afraid," the priest responded simply, over-looking all the other things Joshua had said. "There are troubles here and my own people are being drawn into them. There is another priest who comes into town stirring up the people. I've tried all my life to help my people to avoid hatred and to always forgive, but this man is undoing it all. I've told the bishop about him, but the bishop told me he can't do a thing with him. He's his own man, and the bishop is reluctant to censure him, feeling it won't do any good. And what is even more frightening, a bogus Presbyterian minister also comes through town agitating the Protestants. I have nightmares about the future."

Then the priest, realizing that he had just poured his heart out to a total stranger, remarked to Joshua, "Why do I tell you, a stranger, about problems I've never shared with anyone, not even the bishop?"

Joshua smiled. "Maybe because you feel you can trust me." They both laughed.

"Well, son," the old priest sighed, and picked up his cup and put it in the sink. Joshua did the same, and the two men walked back out into the garden. Marie stood at the door watching Joshua. She had heard the whole conversation and was wondering about this gentle stranger who seemed to understand so much.

Joshua thanked the priest for his kindness and told him God was pleased with the work he had done during such troubled times and would soon answer his prayers. The priest didn't pay much attention to what Joshua was saying, not having the slightest hint as to who he was. But he thanked Joshua for listening and welcomed him back whenever he wished to come. If he would like to come to supper, he would be most welcome anytime. Joshua thanked him and left.

The old man went back to his garden, watching Joshua as he walked up the road, thinking what a strange young man he was.

CHAPTER 8

T

HE WALK to the nearest city was invigorating. Joshua liked to walk. It was ordinary travel in his time, and he did a lot of thinking while walking. There were berry bushes along the way; he picked the juicy berries and ate them by the handful. They weren't very filling, but they were tasty and nourishing. Cars drove past, and every now and then someone would stop and offer him a lift. Joshua declined politely. Then, when he was almost halfway to the city, a car stopped and the driver offered him a ride. Joshua readily accepted, as if he had been waiting for this person all along.

He got into the car and the driver introduced himself. His name was John Hourihan, a sturdily built man in his forties, with thick, straight, jet-black hair. He was soft-spoken and said little during the ride, but he listened to Joshua, trying to analyze this stranger he had never seen before.

John was headmaster at a school in the city, and though he was Catholic he managed to persuade the trustees of the school to open its doors to children of all religions. It was a bold move for the time and place but it accomplished much in fostering a better feeling among the children for one another. John mentioned that some of the children from his school had been in the village square in the morning and told of a stranger they had met there, and that they were fascinated by him because he was different. Joshua asked if they were pleased with the stranger, and did his meeting with them make them happy, and did they like his guitar playing. John began to realize his rider may have been that stranger, so he asked him.

"Yes, it was I," Joshua replied simply. "I wanted to bring the children a little happiness. They seemed so heavy-hearted for such little children."

"Yes, it's sad," John commented, "to think that joy should be stripped from their lives even before they get a chance to live. That's why in my school we try to bring the children together in a relaxed atmosphere so they can get to know one another. We had problems in the beginning, and threats from some sick people, but things have been working out well. We have a good number of really good children, strong kids, the type who will be leaders one day."

They reached the city limits, and John asked Joshua where he wanted to be dropped off. Joshua told him near the city park.

"I don't know your name," John said to Joshua.

"Joshua," he replied, "just Joshua."

The park wasn't far away. John stopped the car and let out his passenger.

"Good luck, Joshua. Hope to see you again."

"Thank you very much for the ride. We will meet again."

Joshua walked down the street toward the park. John drove off, watching him through the mirror, still wondering about him.

The park was filling with people, and Joshua walked to the edge of the crowd. They looked intense, humorless. He had seen people like that before. He felt uncomfortable but walked on, mingling with a loose gathering of people who had entered the park with him. It was twelve twenty-five; the event was to start at twelve-thirty. A raised platform at the back of the tree-lined park was decorated with orange and white bunting and flags of various organizations. It was festive and dramatic in contrast with the greens and browns of the trees and lawn and the rather drab colors of the people's clothes. Many in the crowd were workmen on their lunch hour; others had come from a distance for the occasion, to hear this electrifying orator they had either heard before or heard about.

A stir rippled across the crowd, and a breathless silence ensued. A course-looking, bull-like man mounted the platform and was introduced as the great evangelist of their day, the Reverend John V. Maislin, to the wild acclaim of the crowd. After the seemingly endless applause, the speaker motioned for silence and began to speak:

"My good people, and I call you good because you have sacrificed your time and your lunch hour to be here with me on this hot summer day. You are here because you fear the Lord and you want to listen to the truth, the truth that sets us free, as the Lord has promised. We are in danger of losing that freedom, for the enemy is in our midst. He is right here mingling in the crowd with you today. He is the wolf in sheep's clothing, waiting for a chance to ravage and rape you good, God-fearing people. And that enemy is the Antichrist, the Pope, and his bloodthirsty emissaries, who are everywhere, trying to strip from you your freedom, your hard-won democracy.

"Democracy is the product of the Reformation. Rome had kept people enslaved for centuries, and would do so today if we let them. There are forces all around us today who would, if they could, strip us of our precious freedom. These are the secret collaborators of the Vatican dictators. Some of these evil and vicious people cloak themselves in the guise of Protestant bishops, as strange as that may seem.

"I speak to you as a friend. I stand between you and God and I speak to you from God. I have known God, and I speak to you as a prophet from God. I am concerned for you because of forces unleashed in the world today. Churches trying to unite is the work of Satan. It goes counter to all we stand for as Protestants. And everyone is falling for it, from the Archbishop of Canterbury to the Orthodox Patriarchs, who can't wait for the right time to team up with the Antichrist in Rome. That is because they are the leaders of churches that hate the Bible and teach their people the doctrines of men, the height of idolatry.

"I am warning you, my dear people, like the prophets tried to warn the Jews of old, that these enemies are all around us. Their followers are planning right now to strip your freedom from you and turn you back into bondage. We must fight them with every weapon at our disposal until we destroy the Satan in our midst."

A group of the preacher's henchmen had been watching Joshua all during the talk and could tell he did not approve of what their leader was saying. They walked over to him as he stood at the edge of the crowd and, confronting him, asked bluntly, "Don't you agree with the preacher?"

Joshua looked at them, unintimidated, and spoke very calmly. "God is love and what is of God never preaches hate. By their fruits you shall know them. The fruit of hatred is suspicion of one's neighbors, even of one's own family, and violence. Violence does not come from God.

There is enough hatred and violence in the world without clergy preaching hatred. They are the true wolves in sheep's clothing, the true Antichrist, preaching the exact opposite of everything Jesus taught. Everyone is a child of God, and everyone is searching for God in his or her own way. People are not evil, and God's true shepherds preach love and forgiveness and forbearance in the face of injustice, never hatred and suspicion of one's neighbor. That is the work of the devil."

"You're a bloody papist, you bastard," said one of the hired thugs as he hauled off and hit Joshua straight in the jaw. Joshua looked at him calmly, unperturbed, like long ago when the servant of the high priest did the same thing.

The calm, fearless look in Joshua's eyes unsteadied the thug. He knew the stranger was not afraid of him, but for some reason, far beyond his retarded comprehension, he refused to react . . . and not from fear. The man felt a twinge of guilt, because he saw no hatred in Joshua's eyes, only pity. He walked away ashamed. His companion followed him.

People standing near were shocked but unsympathetic, because they were all of the same ilk, and they assumed that what the preacher's thugs did was totally justified though they didn't understand it.

Joshua now knew what he was facing. The battle lines were clear. A strategy was slowly taking shape in his mind.

He walked away from the crowd and started on his trek back to the village.

CHAPTER 9

IT WAS only a few miles back to the village. Joshua's jaw ached, but he tried not to pay attention to it. Not many cars were traveling in the direction of the village, but a farmer was driving his horse and farm wagon in Joshua's direction so he offered him a lift. Joshua hopped on the wagon and the two men rode down the highway.

"My name's Tommy. What's yours?" the farmer said in friendly fashion as he offered his hand to Joshua.

"Joshua," he responded.

"I saw what happened back there at the park when I was driving by. That preacher does the work of the devil. I'm Protestant myself, but I don't go for the likes of him and that crew with him. All they do is stir up trouble. Our village was friendly for years. Catholics and Protestants got along good until that fellow and his henchmen started coming to town, arousing fear and suspicion in people. I saw that fellow hit you back there. Why didn't you punch him back? You look strong enough to take care of yourself."

"Fighting has no meaning for me. Animals fight because they lack the intelligence to solve problems in any other way. For me it would have accomplished nothing.

It's better to avoid those kinds of people," Joshua answered quietly.

"Where are you staying in town?" the farmer asked as he sucked on his pipe.

"No place in particular."

The farmer sensed Joshua was just one of those daydreaming wanderers and could see he was harmless, so he invited him to stay at their farmhouse. It wasn't much, but at least he would have a place to lay his head. It was lonely at the farm since their son left for America a few months before.

Joshua accepted.

Tommy was in his late sixties and was used to long hours of work each day. Even though it was only midafternoon, he had already done a good day's work and was on his way home after dropping off his produce at the market.

As the wagon approached the village a few of the children recognized Joshua and laughed with delight at seeing him on the old farm wagon, waving to him and calling him as the wagon rolled by.

Joshua waved to them. Two of the boys ran alongside the wagon, asking Joshua if he was going to be in the square the next morning.

"Yes, I'll be there. Bring your friends with you and we will have a good time."

"What was that all about?" Tom asked his rider.

"I've been meeting with the children in the village square. They are trying to teach me how to play the trumpet and a few other things. It's good for them, keeps them out of trouble."

The wagon continued through town, and the few

people walking down the street waved hello to Tommy. He was a fixture in the neighborhood and everyone liked him and his wife, Millie. They were kind, gentle people who bothered no one and always lent a hand when someone needed them.

Tom did not have to steer the horse up Stonecastle Road. Old Willie knew the route by instinct. Even blindfolded he could travel the road from the farm to the market and back home. As they approached the farm the horse's pace speeded up. He knew his oats would be in a little pile at the entrance to the small corral.

Joshua helped Tommy unhitch the horse and unload the wagon. They went up to the house together. Millie met them at the door and relieved Joshua of some of the packages. Coming into the kitchen, Tommy introduced Joshua to his wife and told her all about the incident at Rev. Maislin's rally.

Millie was a thin, wiry woman in her early sixties. Her face was shaped like a leprechaun's, which her quaintly pointed nose accentuated. When she smiled, as she did when her husband introduced her to Joshua, she radiated good humor and a jolly spirit.

Joshua had a good time that evening. Their supper was ordinary simple fare, but the good humor and happy spirits were in tune with Joshua's own free spirit. Tommy told Joshua about their pastor at the Presbyterian church and said he would like Joshua to meet him some evening, and if it would be acceptable to their guest, he would invite the pastor and his wife for supper.

Joshua thought that a great idea and said he would look forward to the occasion, as there were many things he would like to discuss with the pastor.

After supper Joshua insisted on helping his hosts with their tasks around the farm, and when everything was done they spent a few relaxing moments sitting on the porch enjoying the cool evening breeze and watching the birds gliding across the evening sky in the setting sun.

CHAPTER 10

THE VILLAGE SQUARE was quiet early in the morning. The only people there were workers on their way to their jobs, lunch boxes in hand and a spring in their steps, some whistling happy tunes, some not so happy. Joshua greeted each one as he passed, and all without exception returned the good wishes. Before coming to the square Joshua had helped Tommy ready himself for his daily trip to the market, and after breakfast had ridden with him as far as the square.

Joshua sat on the wall, sometimes looking across the square, sometimes letting his gaze wander across the meadow. It was melancholy and peaceful this time of day. The shadows were long. The air was clean. The sun was soft. It was quiet. Joshua liked quiet.

It wasn't long after most of the workers had left the village that Jane walked down into the square to perform her daily ritual. All the birds in creation were waiting for her. As soon as she opened the bag they besieged her, one landing on her shoulder, another on her wrist. She scattered the seed along the pavement as she made her way toward Joshua. The flurry of flying birds distracted him. When he turned and saw the little girl walking toward him, he smiled.

"Good morning, Joshua!"

"Good morning, little one! Those birds surely do like you."

"That's because I feed them every day. If I didn't feed them, they wouldn't even come near me."

"They know you love them. You show them that by feeding them. During the summer it's good to skip some days, so they get used to looking for their own food. It's better for them. They need you more in the cold winter, when food is scarce."

"Joshua, do you think you can get the cardinal to come to me again?" Jane asked him.

They both looked up into the tree. He was there waiting, watching.

"Give me a handful of seed," Joshua said as he extended his hand.

He held his hand out toward the bird. After a little hesitation, the bird flew down, looked up at Joshua, then at Jane, and started to eat. The girl slowly took some seed from the bag and gently moved her hand closer to Joshua's, just like on the previous occasion. When the bird had finished the seed in Joshua's hand, he stopped, looked up, hopped onto Jane's hand, and started to eat. The girl was delighted and tried to contain her joy, so as not to frighten the nervous creature. When he had finished he flew back into the tree.

Children began filtering into the square earlier than usual. This time they were not the same children who had been with Joshua the day before. They were kids from the group who had stood at a distance and watched the others playing with Joshua. As they began to gather they looked over at Joshua talking with the girl. They wanted to approach him but were hesitant. Joshua noticed and made a friendly gesture toward them. They responded immedi-

ately by starting to walk across the square. Jane looked
frightened. Joshua put his hand on her shoulder to
reassure her and told her not to be afraid. "Stay here with
me and don't be afraid," he said to her. She relaxed and
clung close to her friend, though she wanted to run away
at seeing all those strange kids coming. They were Protestants.

As the children began to encircle Joshua and the girl,
Joshua told them his name and also introduced Jane. She
tried to be friendly. The oldest boy in the group immediately took charge and introduced his friends. After giving
the names of all the others, he introduced himself. "My
name is John Clark." They all rather embarrassedly said
hello.

John was about thirteen years old. He was not very tall,
but was stocky and solid and had thick curly hair. He
asked Joshua where he was from and why he had come to
their village. Joshua answered, then asked them about
themselves, and about school, and about their play. One of
the children had a rubber ball. Joshua asked him if he
could borrow it. The boy gladly gave it to him. Joshua took
it and covered it with his hand. When he opened his hands
a frog jumped out onto the pavement. The kids screamed
with delight. One of the boys picked up the frog and gave
it back to Joshua, asking him how he did it. Joshua smiled
and took the frog. He threw it up in the air and it began to
fly away. It had become a sparrow. After circling the
square, and diving down toward the kids, the bird flew
back to Joshua and landed on his hand. The children were
beside themselves. They had heard about magicians but
had never seen one in action.

At about that point the other group of children, who
had been with Joshua previously, entered the square.

They were surprised to see their friend playing with Protestant kids. At first they were offended. Joe felt the worst. He felt betrayed, but then remarked to the others, "He was our friend first. What difference does it make if the other kids like him too? Why should we stay away?"

Many of the children were reluctant to mingle with the Protestant group, but when Joe walked over the others followed. As they moved closer they saw what Joshua was doing and they, too, were fascinated. The bird had just flown back to Joshua and had landed on his hand as a rubber ball. Joshua took the ball and threw it over the heads of the children near him to Joe. When he saw it coming Joe quickly put his trumpet down and caught the ball. As he did it turned into a little rabbit. In shock, he dropped it, then stooped down, picked it up, together with his trumpet, and brought it over to Joshua. The kids had heard of magicians doing tricks like that but had never witnessed it. Was it an illusion? Was he just playing tricks with their imagination or was what they were seeing really happening?

Joshua continued playing with the children in this manner for the better part of an hour, coming up with an endless display of tricks, gradually drawing the children more and more into the action until, having forgotten themselves, they were all mingling and having fun together, something they had never done before—Catholics and Protestants playing and laughing and talking to one another and having a perfectly good time. It was unheard of. Before it all ended Joe was teaching one of the Protestant boys how to play the trumpet.

CHAPTER 11

THAT NIGHT Joshua slept under the big tree in the meadow. It was a warm night with a delicious breeze, and no mosquitoes or troubling insects, so it was a perfect place to sleep. It was Joshua's chosen place of repose. He liked being alone at night, as in times past, when he would go off into the hills by himself, while his companions retired to their cozy, comfortable homes. "The birds of the air have their nests, the foxes have their dens, but the son of man has nowhere to lay his head." There weren't any tall mountains or big hills nearby, but the meadow was isolated and quiet, and it wasn't far from the brook that snaked through the fields, so it was a good place to gather one's thoughts and just relax.

The next day all the children gathered with Joshua. They were a little uncomfortable at first, but Joshua broke the ice by beckoning them all to come closer. After a few minutes they were all relaxed. He repeated some of the tricks he had performed the day before for the benefit of new kids the others had brought. Joshua asked each one his or her name, which, to the children's surprise, he was never to forget. He would even at times call by name children he had not met before, which really shocked them. The children didn't stay too long but said they would come back the next day if Joshua would be there.

He said he would. After all the other children left, Joe stayed on at the square with Joshua, helping him to master the trumpet. When he left, a little after noon, he told Joshua to wait for him, he would be back. He did come back, a short time later, with a brown bag full of things to eat. Joe was thoughtful and noticed that Joshua didn't have much of anything and thought he might appreciate some things to nibble on when he got hungry. He was right. Had it not been for his thoughtfulness, Joshua would have gone to sleep that night with an empty stomach. Sitting under the tree in the restful quiet of the early evening, only a few feet from the rippling water, Joshua ate his supper, looking pensively toward the village square, dreaming about times past and things to come.

There was no one to be seen, either in the square or across the meadow. A few sheep wandered by, took a drink in the brook, looked over at the strange being sitting under the tree, and walked away. Joshua didn't bother to call them. He just watched. A cow crossed the stream, walked close to where Joshua was sitting, and mooed quietly. Joshua called the animal. She looked over, curious, and walked closer. Joshua held out his hand to the animal. The cow smelled the salt he was holding and came over and licked it out of his hand. Joshua petted her. She turned and walked away.

As the sun went down, Joshua looked across the horizon, and for a few brief minutes his lips moved as if in silent prayer. He lay down on the warm grass, and in a few minutes was in a deep sleep.

CHAPTER 12

JOSHUA rose early the next morning to the singing of the birds. He wandered across the meadow, drinking in the clean, fresh morning air, then headed toward the square and turned down Maple Street.

The streets were empty except for a few men who went to work early. As Joshua approached St. Mary's church he saw Father Donnelly in his black cassock, walking through the garden, reading his morning prayers, and every now and then inspecting his roses.

"Good morning, Father," Joshua called.

"Good morning, son," the old priest replied in a cheerful tone, obviously glad, though surprised, to see Joshua so early in the day.

The morning Angelus bell was ringing, calling the people to prayer and announcing that morning Mass was about to begin.

"I'm just finishing my morning prayers. Would you like to read the last psalm with me?" the priest asked Joshua.

"Yes, I would. Which one is it?" Joshua asked.

"The Twenty-fifth." The priest intoned the first verse, " 'To you, O Lord, I lift up my soul. My God, in you I trust, and I shall not be shamed.' "

To the priest's surprise, Joshua took up the second

verse without reading it in the priest's book: " 'Do not let my enemies laugh at me, for those who cling to you will never be defeated.' "

" 'Direct me in your truth, and teach me; for you are God my savior, and I look to you all the day long.' "

" 'The Lord is gentle and upright; he sustains those who are stumbling along the way.' "

The two men continued the ancient prayer, and while walking into the church Father Donnelly invited Joshua to stay for Mass, then went up to the sacristy to vest, leaving Joshua in the church.

He took a seat halfway up the aisle. There was a good crowd in the church, almost sixty people, quite a few for only a weekday service. They were mostly women, but there was a handful of men, even younger men, with strong, ruddy features. Many of the women were saying their rosaries, the men just kneeling, absorbed in their thoughts. Joshua knelt straight, with hands clasped. It was always a beautiful sight, watching Joshua at prayer. There was a calmness, a peace, a serenity, and a manliness about Joshua praying that would touch even the most cynical hearts.

The priest emerged from the sacristy and began the Mass. Morning Mass was brief; there were no long sermons like on Sunday. Father Donnelly did make a few comments on the Gospel, about the gentleness and under-standing of Jesus. He went about every day doing good, healing, counseling, comforting, and nowhere, except in one place, does anyone ever thank him. In spite of the people's ingratitude, Jesus never stopped doing good. It is a lesson that his followers need today more than ever before. There is so much hurt and misery, and so many wounds to be healed. We have to adopt the forgiving nature of Jesus, who never allowed himself to take offense, so we can, each in his own way, reach out to heal the hurts all around us. It is our children who will ultimately reap the benefits of our goodness, because one day they will have a better world to live in.

At Communion time Joshua did not go up to receive the Eucharist. The priest noticed and looked down in his direction, quietly inviting him. He still did not go.

After Mass the priest brought his guest to the parish house and insisted he have breakfast with him. The two men enjoyed each other's company, and at one point Father Donnelly told Joshua he was welcome to come to Communion if he liked.

Joshua could see it was perplexing to the priest why this obviously good man refrained from receiving the Eucharist. "Father, did Jesus take Communion at the Last Supper?" he asked the priest.

"No, but that was because the Eucharist was the gift of himself to his followers," the priest replied.

"And so I share in the Eucharist in the same way. You will understand one day. I do believe in this beautiful gift of God."

It was too much for the old priest to grasp, but he was content to know that Joshua did believe in the Eucharist. He told Joshua that it was a beautiful thing he was doing for the children in the town. Joshua smiled and told the priest that children have the right to grow up happy and free of their parents' hatreds and prejudices. It is a terrible sin for mothers and fathers to teach their children to hate. It would be better if they were drowned in the depths of the sea than to go before God with that sin on their consciences.

"Joshua, I do worry about you. You are a kind man,

and I wonder if you realize how complicated the troubles are here. What you are doing is beautiful. It goes right to the heart of the problem, but because it does it is so easy for you to make a mistake and give sick people the excuse they look for to commit some terrible evil. Be careful."

"My Father is with me in all I do and I will be careful. What I am doing is carefully planned and it will accomplish its purpose. My Father will not be frustrated."

When the two men finished breakfast, the priest told Joshua he had heard he had no place to stay. If that were true, he was welcome to stay in the parish house. Joshua thanked him but said it would be better for him to stay by himself, though he would appreciate it if he could stay at the parish house when it rained. He would very much like to be able to stay at a Protestant home on occasions, too, when the weather was bad. The priest offered to contact his friend Rev. Davis, the Presbyterian minister, and make the suggestion to him.

"I am sure he would be delighted for you to stay at his house. We have already had discussions about you, and I was supposed to invite you to dinner with us sometime soon."

"That would be fun," Joshua said.

"Before you leave, Joshua, you might want to use one of the bathrooms upstairs. Here's a bathrobe. You can leave your clothes outside the door and the housekeeper will wash them for you. They will be ready in no time."

The hot bath felt good. The clothes were cleaned and quickly ironed, so Joshua did not have long to wait. After thanking the priest and the housekeeper, he left. The priest walked him through the garden. The old man had found a friend in Joshua. As a result of his training in the seminary, he had never made friends with parishioners. It was not a good practice. He was father to all of them, so they all felt close to him because he had no favorites. Now that his own family were dead and what few living friends he had were so far away, life was lonely for this simple old man. And even though he was a holy man, it did not make up for the real human need for companionship. In finding Joshua he found in him a rare goodness that embodied all the ideals he had believed in and tried all his life to preach. Meeting this strange young man was perhaps the most rewarding experience of his life. He could talk to him about anything and Joshua would understand, and would have insights that went far beyond what his young years seemed to warrant.

Joshua walked down the street, and the priest wandered around his garden, smelling the lavender that bordered the rosebed.

13

THE CHILDREN were already in the square when Joshua arrived. They were all talking together, Protestants and Catholics. Joshua was happy. It showed on his face. One of the Protestant girls noticed it and remarked to him about it. "I am happy to see you all together," was Joshua's response. "It is the way God's children should be."

The crowd was growing too large to continue meeting in the square. Joshua suggested they walk out into the meadow and gather on the hillside. The kids were all excited with the turn this little adventure in their lives was taking. They scrambled over the stone wall and through the trees. Some walked around the wall and followed the path into the meadow. They gathered on the knoll looking toward the village, which was a good distance away. It was quiet in the meadow, with trees here and there sheltering birds of various descriptions, not unlike similar scenes of long ago.

Joe came up to Joshua and offered his trumpet. Joshua humorously played a simple melody Joe had taught him. It was obvious he didn't take his playing too seriously. The children enjoyed watching him. That was a lesson in itself, Joshua's relaxed, casual attitude.

Some of the other children brought musical instruments. Joshua suggested they get together and form a little orchestra and play for the group. At first they were a little embarrassed, but the idea was a good one, and after a while they were playing well together. Before long the other children were singing along with them. Joshua didn't know the songs at first, but before long he knew them all and sang right along with the children.

When the musicians stopped for a break, one of the boys asked Joshua if he would do tricks again for them, like the day before. The boy with the rubber ball offered his ball to Joshua. He laughed. The boy threw the ball to him and he caught it and threw it way up into the air. It started to fly away. The children looked up, trying to follow the bird as it soared through the sky. A thumping sound at the back of the group distracted the children nearby. They turned and saw the ball bouncing around the field. They looked up into the sky for the bird and couldn't find it. They were still mystified at what was really happening. Did Joshua turn the ball into a bird or was it just an illusion? Some of the kids asked Joshua what really happened. He wouldn't tell them. He just smiled coyly and said to them, "You see, things are not necessarily what they appear to be. Always watch what happens and try to understand. There are strange things in life that look attractive on the surface but underneath can cause you harm. Do not be taken in by nice words or deceptive ideas. Think about them in the quiet of your nights, and when you are worried talk to God and ask him for understanding. The devil still wanders around in sheep's clothing, trying to deceive God's little ones. Always be careful."

The children enjoyed listening to Joshua speak like this. He spoke so gently, not like parents and other grown-ups, who are usually harsh and dogmatic and critical with children. His words were soothing and tranquil.

A little girl, considerably younger than the other children, was standing close to Joshua. She was wearing a pink dress decorated with forget-me-nots. Joshua noticed her looking down at the ground. She seemed sad. He reached down, picked a wildflower that was only in bud, and handed it to the girl. Her eyes sparkled as the bud began to open up right in front of her eyes. The other children asked Joshua to do the same thing for them. Joshua laughed. He knew he had put himself into a predicament.

He told all the children to pick a wildflower in bud. They scampered in all directions, looking for the kind they liked. When they were ready Joshua told them to be very quiet and concentrate and really believe. One by one the buds began to open. Only one little boy's did not open. He was standing not too far from Joshua. When he saw that everyone else's had opened, he began to cry and tried to hide his tears. Joshua saw him and called him over. He bent down and put his arm around his shoulders and asked the boy his name.

"My name is Kevin."

"How old are you?"

"Seven."

"Why did your bud not open?"

Through his tears the boy told Joshua, "I didn't think it would happen, but now I know."

"Take the bud home with you and see what happens," Joshua told him.

"Will it open?"

"You will see."

Joshua then told the group to sit down on the grass in small groups. They did as he told them.

When they were seated and quiet, Joshua leaned against a huge boulder, half sitting on it, half leaning against it, and began to tell the children a story.

"A young boy dreamed of being a great musician. He practiced hours each day and thought of nothing else but becoming famous and very wealthy. He knew the kind of music people liked and the kind that would make him rich, so he learned to write and perform music that pleased people, and it was not always good music. It was music about pleasure and wordly games and revolution and drugs. Young people liked his music and it became the popular music of the time. He had left home and lost contact with his family, especially his younger brother, who had loved and admired and missed him very much. He, too, missed his little brother and thought about him on lonely nights when his friends were busy about other things. He wondered what had happened to him. He hadn't heard from him in so long.

"Not long afterward the older brother was invited to a surprise party, the kind he was accustomed to attending. There were many people there he didn't know, mingling among a handful of his friends. Late in the evening one of the guests started to read poems, poems like the lyrics in the musician's songs. They were not good poems, but cheap and immoral. Everyone was laughing and enjoying the poems, but laughing more at the young man who was reading them. He was drugged and strange-looking. His dissolute life had destroyed him as a man. The musician felt a strange sense of sadness but couldn't understand why. He asked one of his friends who the young man was who was reading the poems, and his friend was surprised he did not know. That is your brother. He has loved and admired you all your life and spent his whole life imitating what you write about in your music. The musician became sick and left the party in disgust. He had realized too late that he had used the beautiful gifts that God had given him to make money, and in the process had destroyed not only the lives of many people but the life of the brother he had loved so much. It never occurred to him what evil was until he saw what his music had done to this brother's soul.

"Fortunately, that was not the end of the story. The young musician left all his friends and went off by himself to repent. He prayed for God to forgive him and to heal his little brother's tortured soul. He promised that if God would heal his brother, he would write music about beautiful things, and about peace, and about things that would bring joy into this world of darkness and troubled hearts. God heard his prayer and healed his brother. The two became close friends, never again to be separated. The musician composed music that was to inspire millions of people and bring joy and harmony into a world torn apart by selfishness and ambition. The younger brother wrote the words for all his brother's music. And their lives were filled with the kind of peace and happiness that God gives to those who find Him and who bring his joy into others' lives.

"Each one of you is like that musician. You have rare gifts that God has given you, to bring an important message to those around you. God has given each of you something special that he wants you to share with others. You can see already the beautiful things God can work among you if you let him. A few days ago you were strangers. You never thought you would be friends. Today you are friends. You help each other. You teach each other, like Joe and his new friend playing the trumpet together. You share with each other. And you have a peace you never knew possible. That peace and that friendship can continue for many years and can change the lives of all around you, and can create a beautiful world for your children to live in. That is the beauty of God's love."

All during Joshua's talk the children sat spellbound, drinking in every word, some with tears flowing down their cheeks. When he finished they all stood up and spontaneously turned to each other and hugged one another, the only fitting conclusion to the touching story Joshua had just told them.

It was almost lunchtime when Joshua finished his story. He sent the children off and told them he would see them in the square the following morning. Joe and the friend he was teaching to play the trumpet accompanied Joshua across the meadow. Joe asked Joshua if he was talking about him in the story. Joshua told him that every individual has a decision to make, either to live his life for himself or to live his life as a partner with God. One day he will have to make that decision, and he should always remember that story.

As they approached the square Joe and his friend said good-bye to Joshua and sat down on an odd-shaped tree with an almost horizontal trunk. It was trumpet-lesson time for Joe's friend. Joshua continued his way through the square and up Stonecastle Road.

14

JOSHUA spent the rest of the day by himself, wandering around the Protestant section of town, greeting people in his open, friendly manner. Many people in town already knew Joshua by reputation, so the people along Stonecastle Road recognized him from the children's description. Most were friendly, although some seemed wary.

The view from upper Stonecastle Road was magnificent. You could see for miles across the meadow, and on a clear day you could even see the ocean in the distance. Joshua walked out on a high knoll overlooking the village and the meadow and sat down on a rock to gaze out on the vast scenery before him. It was a peaceful spot, the kind that always appealed to him.

"Like that scenery, young man?" spoke a voice that startled Joshua and broke his silent meditation. He turned and saw a man dressed in a black clerical suit standing next to him. He was in his early fifties, thin, and, though a bit proper, radiated an affable kind of friendliness. Joshua assumed he was one of the village ministers.

"Yes, it's a beautiful site, and so restful. It's almost like a window into heaven," Joshua responded in friendly fashion.

"My name is Russell Davis. I'm minister at that

church behind us across the street. I noticed you walking up the hill as I was coming from the post office. I think I already know you. One of my parishioners told me about you, the one who picked you up on the highway a few days ago. You're Joshua, aren't you?"

"Yes," Joshua replied as he stood up to shake the cleric's hand. "Word travels fast in the village, doesn't it?"

"Our place is small and there are few distractions, so every little event is news. Besides, you have become more than just an event. It seems the whole town is buzzing about you. I've heard from quite a few of my parishioners about what you have been doing with the children, and I think it's great. In fact, it seems almost miraculous. I hope it can continue. I just bumped into my friend Father Donnelly down at the post office. He told me you had been over to visit with him and said you would like to stay at the manse on occasion. I told him I felt honored, and I mean that, Joshua. You are more than welcome to stay at our home whenever you like. You are like a breath of fresh air to our village, and we are all so grateful for what you are doing for our children. Two of my own children are now among your "disciples" and they fill us in on everything you do. I didn't mean to interrupt your meditation, but I couldn't resist meeting you. In fact, I'm just going home for a bite to eat. I'd be delighted if you'd come home with me and have lunch."

Joshua did not get a chance to say much, but he was encouraged by the friendliness of the minister. "Yes, I would like that. I have to admit I am quite hungry."

The two men walked out of the little park, across the street, and up the long drive to the manse, talking excitedly about many things. Approaching the house, Joshua commented about how beautifully the minister kept his grounds. "You tend your gardens and lawns with such care. I'm sure it's a reflection of the care you have for your flock. The gardens are beautiful. Do you work them yourself?"

"Sometimes. I like to work in the garden, but I have all I can do to keep up with my people. We don't live in easy times, and I mingle with the people as much as possible, trying to help them steer a sensible course through all the troubles we have here. I'm sure Father Donnelly has already told you we used to have a peaceful village with Protestants and Catholics getting along well together until agitators came into town and started stirring up trouble and arousing suspicions and fears that had been laid to rest years ago.

"I don't know whether you've heard, but just a few nights ago there was trouble out on the coast, which, as you could see, is not very far from the village. I learned about it from Father Donnelly. No one has the straight story, but rumor has it that a boat full of arms landed and the Arab guerrillas who delivered the shipment had a young boy with them whose family lives in the vicinity. They were dropping him off to be picked up by his parents. While switching the cargo from the boat into trucks, the boy was careless and set off a small explosion, which left him blind. By the time troops arrived to investigate the reported explosion, the band had already slipped away. The boy himself had been smuggled back home and was being cared for secretly in the Catholic section of the city."

The inside of the manse was tastefully decorated with Queen Anne furniture and an assortment of antiques. Joshua admired the quality of the craftsmanship.

Hearing voices in the foyer, a woman came out to see who was there. The minister turned and saw his wife standing in the doorway and introduced her to Joshua. "Kathie, this is Joshua, the man the whole town is talking about. I just picked him up loitering in our park."

The woman walked over to the two men and Rev. Davis continued with the introductions. "Joshua, this is my loyal and devoted friend, Kathie. She is also my wife."

At that point his daughter came in, a young girl in her early teens, a pretty, quick-witted girl named Meredith. He introduced her to Joshua, who smiled a warm hello.

After exchanging courtesies, the girl left and the three went into the kitchen to continue their conversation over samplings of Kathie's cooking.

Joshua did not stay long at the manse, but the two men discussed issues that deeply concerned them both. They also made tentative plans for dinner with Father Donnelly. After Joshua left the Reverend Davis had the same peaceful and comforted feeling from his meeting with Joshua that the priest had experienced. He felt reassured and had the sense of being in the presence of a rare goodness that he had never experienced before. Kathie agreed and suggested they invite him over often.

15

J ANE, the little girl who first met Joshua, was feeling left out with all the excitement she had created among her friends over Joshua. She used to be able to meet him in the square while feeding the birds and have him all to herself, but he hadn't been there lately, so it was only among her crowd of friends that she got to see him. She was just one of a large group now, lost in the crowd. She felt hurt and hoped Joshua didn't forget her. She had hoped he would be in the square this morning when she went to feed the birds, but he wasn't. She was heartbroken and walked around the streets looking for him. He was nowhere. When he showed up later it was too late. The crowd of kids had gathered, and she couldn't even get near him. She had seen him later, after the crowd had broken up, as he was walking up Stonecastle Road. She wanted to follow him but didn't because that part of town was forbidden for Catholics. She just stood at a distance and watched him disappear from sight.

But the next morning she was all excited to see him in the square when she went about her daily ritual, which she had almost forgotten to do in her excitement.

"Joshua, Joshua," she called out to him, and came running over to him, with all the birds in creation chasing after their breakfast. When she reached him she lost her tongue and stood there speechless. Joshua bent down and reached out, holding her hands in his. He could see all the feelings running through her and tried to reassure her he hadn't forgotten her.

"It has been a long time since we talked," he said to her softly, "but I haven't forgotten you. I see you in the crowd with the other children, and I am happy you brought them all to me. I am your good friend always. I want you to remember that. You are very special to me—"

"But, Joshua," she interrupted, "there is another friend I want you to meet. His name is Patrick. He doesn't come with the others. He was hurt by a bomb and is afraid to go outside his house anymore. I told him all about you, and he wants so much to see you. Could you come with me to his house?"

Joshua smiled. "Yes, I think we could do that. Where does he live?"

"Not far, I'll show you. Come with me," she said as the two walked down the street.

She took her friend down Maple Street and, turning off the main street, stopped at a modest, whitewashed stone cottage.

"This is where he lives," Jane said, knocking at the thick wooden door. It was opened almost immediately by a young woman with reddish-brown hair. The woman looked tense and sad.

"Hello, Mrs. Whitehead," Janie said. "I brought my friend Joshua so Pat could meet him."

Still bitter over her daughter's murder and her son's incessant nightmares, Maureen was none too excited about letting a stranger into her house. "I've heard about you. What good can you do in this hell we live in?" she said cynically. "You can't bring my Annie back. And you certainly can't change these sick bastards, hell-bent on killing innocent children."

Jane was horrified at what came out of the woman's mouth. She was embarrassed for Joshua, who didn't seem the slightest bit upset. It was Maureen who was ashamed and shocked at her own behavior, and she apologized to Joshua and the little girl for her lack of courtesy and her emotional outburst.

"Please come inside. I can't imagine why I was so rude."

Patrick was sitting on the floor putting a puzzle together. When he saw Janie he got off the floor and walked over to her. "Hi, Janie!"

"Hi, Pat! I brought my friend Joshua to visit you. I told him you don't go out much."

The boy looked up at Joshua. Then he looked down at his heavily bandaged arm.

"Hello, Patrick! That is a good name you have. Patrick was a great man. Are you going to be like him?" Joshua asked the boy in an attempt to lighten the atmosphere and start a conversation with the boy.

"I don't think I could be like him. He was a saint," the boy responded.

"Everyone is called to be a saint, each in his own way," Joshua answered. "You are a very special boy, Patrick, and God has something very special for you if you listen to his voice."

The boy wasn't impressed, but he listened. (Someday it would have meaning. That's the way it is with children. They absorb everything and store it away. Later on it registers at a time in their lives when it will be needed.)

"What about my sister, Annie? I think she was special," the boy said, to everyone's surprise.

"Yes, she was special, and she had a special work to do for God. Her goodness and innocence live in everyone's memory, showing them the meanness of violence and the need for peace and love. She shared in Jesus' work, pointing the way to a better world. And as Jesus died so people could have God's love, so Annie died so others could have a better world. Her special work is now accomplished and she is with God, happy and in joy. Even though you can't see her, she is near you all the time, especially when you need her, and when you talk to her she hears you. She is like an angel, more beautiful than you can imagine."

"How do you know?" the boy asked, still needing reassurance.

"Because I've seen her," Joshua said bluntly.

"You've seen her?" Pat persisted, still not convinced.

"Yes. She is happy and knows everything about you."

"Where is she?"

"In heaven."

"Where is heaven?"

"Heaven is where God is, and God is everywhere, so heaven is everywhere, all around you."

"Why can't I see heaven?"

"Heaven is in a world beyond, just on the other side of a thin veil of time. If you could close your eyes and walk through that veil, you could be there. It is that close," Joshua said, more for Maureen's comfort than for the child's, realizing Pat could not fully understand. He was more impressed with Joshua saying he had seen his sister than by his description of where heaven is.

Maureen had tears in her eyes. She looked at Joshua, wondering about this strange man who could talk about heaven as glibly as a man could talk about his hometown, almost as if he had just come from there. It gave her an eerie feeling, but it also comforted her, hearing this man speak with such conviction.

While Joshua continued talking to the boy and Janie, the mother went to the stove to prepare a pot of tea, asking Joshua if he would like some, which he gladly accepted. She readied a glass of milk and some cookies for the children. Everyone was still standing. Maureen apologized for being so forgetful and offered Joshua a seat at the kitchen table. The children sat down on either side of him.

"Father Donnelly, our parish priest, talked about you at our women's club," Maureen said as she took the tea off the stove to let it steep. "Some of the women were concerned about you and what you were up to. He told them not to fear, that you were a good man and we could be comfortable letting our children be with you. I can see now. But I can't help but think you are very naive to think you can change things around here. There's too much hatred and fear."

"Fear comes from not knowing, and hatred comes from fear of being threatened," Joshua said calmly. "A willingness to understand is the first step in banishing fear. As understanding grows, fear diminishes, and hatred turns to trust. It can happen if people genuinely want peace. In these troubled times people owe it to their children to take the first step. It is unfortunate that men who pose as instruments of God are the very ones who are doing the work of Satan by preaching hatred and suspicion among God's children. They are the real satans, doing their father's work, but the people must not listen to them, because true men of God never preach hatred but try to heal and draw God's children together."

Joshua stayed only a few minutes longer after finishing the tea and cookies. Before leaving he placed his hand on

Pat's head, and for a brief moment closed his eyes and prayed silently. Tears began to roll down the boy's cheeks. His mother asked him why he was crying.

"Because I feel so good. I feel so happy," the boy replied, not knowing what was happening to him.

Then Joshua left, with Jane following him.

"I'm glad you visited Pat," Jane confided to Joshua. "He's been very sad since he was hurt and his sister died. He doesn't want to play with anyone anymore. Your visit made him feel good."

Joshua thanked her for being a good missionary. Jane told him she had to go home, so she left abruptly and skipped down the street. Joshua continued in the direction of the square.

CHAPTER 16

As the days went by Joshua's popularity with the children spread and the crowd that followed him grew larger with each passing day. The night after Joshua visited Pat's house was cause for the greatest joy. It was the first night the boy had been able to sleep undisturbed by haunting dreams and nightmares. It wasn't long afterward that the doctor removed the bandages from the boy's arm, and he was shocked to see that the arm seemed healed and there were no scars. X rays showed no trace of any wounds or injury. He was at a loss to explain the phenomenon to the boy's parents. An even greater consolation for the parents was the fact that their son seemed himself and at peace again. They told the doctor about Joshua visiting their house and blessing the boy. The doctor said nothing. He did call in the other doctors involved in the case and let them examine the boy themselves to see what they made of the boy's condition. The surgeons were delighted with the boy's remarkable healing ability. The psychiatrist found it difficult to understand how the boy could have recovered from the trauma so fast. He was at a loss for an explanation but wondered if it might be just a temporary remission that could give way to a future relapse. Mike and Maureen also wondered. They had their own feelings about what hap-

pened but kept them to themselves. They were happy their
boy was healed.

Sunday came and Joshua attended the Anglican church
services. The people were surprised to see him there, but
were pleased nonetheless. People were curious about him,
as word had spread into practically every household in
town. Most of the parishioners at Christ Church were
friendly. Some were wondering what his ultimate agenda
really was and looked askance at him, analyzing his every
gesture and expression. The more astute realized this
stranger had managed to captivate the total population of
young people in their area—Catholics, Protestants, and
everyone in between. Why? What was his purpose? Some
were beginning to feel concern even if they didn't express
it. Yet, he was a good man, and things the children
brought back home about him were only good, and he was
having a good effect on the way they were treating one
another.

That Sunday afternoon another jarring incident occurred in the village. A Roman Catholic priest by the name
of Father Jack Brown came into town and met with a group
of Catholics outside the village. He was the one Father
Donnelly had told Joshua about. His visits were clandestine, unlike the brash public demonstrations of his Protestant counterpart. The purpose, however, was the
same—to arouse the people and incite them to violence as
the only way they would ever have their freedom. They
had been in bondage long enough. Peaceful means were
not working. Violence was the only route. Joshua didn't
make it to the priest's talk, but heard about it from Tim
McGirr that afternoon when Tim passed Joshua on his
way home through the meadow. Joshua was playing a little
wooden flute he had made. Tim had just left friends he

had stopped off to visit on his way home from Mass a few hours earlier.

The two men sat under the tree for the good part of an hour, talking about pressing issues in the village and the problems of the children. Tim could wax philosophical at times, and this was the time. After he had unwound his spool he invited Joshua to his house for dinner. Joshua accepted and they both walked across the field together.

On the way home Tim told Joshua all about Father Brown. He was a young man, not more than thirty-one, thirty-two. He was gaunt, nervous-looking, reminding one of a high-strung cat. When he spoke his eyes flashed with anger, an unforgiving kind of anger that could frighten people. Not many people listened to him, but those who did were fanatically loyal. He was an embarrassment to most of the Catholics here, who were decent people.

Joshua received a royal welcome this time when he and Tim reached the house, in contrast to the reception the first time he was there. By now his name had spread all over and he was a celebrity. Besides that, the kids missed him. They had all enjoyed his company the last time, but especially Christopher, who beamed now when Joshua came into the house, although he didn't say much.

Tim's mother had been saying her rosary on the front porch when the two came walking up the path. After she had greeted Joshua with a friendly hello, she continued her beads as Tim and Joshua went inside.

Joshua spent the rest of the day at the McGirrs', playing simple games with the kids and talking lightheartedly with the adults until well into the night. Christopher finally felt comfortable enough to ask Joshua if he would play a game of cards with him. They played a few games, until the others got jealous and started looking for attention. Then he went back to including the others in their games.

The McGirr children had heard about Joshua meeting with the children in town although they had not been there themselves. They asked Joshua if they could come too. Stella had some reservations, but when Joshua explained what happened at the meetings, she felt a little easier about letting the children go, even though it meant allowing them to mingle with children from troubled families.

The day began early at the McGirrs', so it was not too late when they turned in for the night.

17

Joshua left early the next morning, walking across the field and up to the meadow on the hill. On his way he stopped at his tree and picked up a bulky brown bag he had hidden there. It was a perfect start of a new day. The sun was warm, and the blue sky was undisturbed except for a few wisps of white floating like sailboats across a blue sea. Birds were singing, and Joshua felt the freedom of nature at peace, though he knew that underneath the surface of the peaceful calm were churning currents anything but peaceful.

He walked to the top of the knoll and surveyed the landscape. He could see almost as far as the ocean. A few small hills in the distance broke the seemingly endless sweep of the thick, deep green carpet that spread as far as the eye could see. Joshua sat down on the grass and it was warm. The sun had burned away the early morning dew. As he looked across the meadow he thought of Capernaum of long ago. This scene was not unlike the hillside up above the ancient city, though the meadow here was greener and the rolling hills more gentle. His prayer was a quiet prayer, mingled with memories, asking peace upon this troubled land of such simple, beautiful people. Joshua's mind saw clearly things far and things near. All was present to his simple but highly complex mind. He knew the way events were unfolding. He and his Father planned it this way. He could see the whole drama, piece by piece fitting into place, all the actors stepping onto the stage at the right time, as if on cue. But it wasn't all predetermined, as if people were just props. Each one's foreseen use of his freedom was carefully considered, providing material in planning the strategy for Joshua's visit to this little corner of the planet.

Joshua sat there on the knoll for well over an hour, most of the time just deep in thought. Suddenly, as if he had come to a long, thoroughly considered decision, he rose and walked through the square, down the street, and in the direction of the city. Children noticed him and ran to ask where he was going.

"To the city," was his reply.

"Can we come?"

"Yes, if you like, and if your parents give you permission."

Word passed rapidly. In no time Joshua's whole coterie of friends was surrounding him, curious as to where they were going and what they were going to do. It was a good five-mile walk to the city, and the thought of going there always thrilled the kids, no matter what the circumstances. They had no money, but these children had no need of money to have fun. They invented their own fun. Joshua admired this trait in them. The simplest little things made them happy.

As they walked along they noticed the bag Joshua was carrying. One of the children, Johnny, a tall, lanky, good-hearted boy who was walking next to Joshua, was dying of curiosity over what was in the bag. No longer able to contain himself, he asked, "Joshua, what do you have in the bag?"

Joshua smiled. "A surprise," he answered.

"What kind of a surprise?" the boy persisted.

By that time they were already past the limits of the village and were next to an open lot strewn with large boulders. Joshua walked into the lot, with the children following him, and told them to sit on the boulders.

There were about twenty-five of them in all, and when they were all settled Joshua opened the bag and emptied its contents on top of one of the rocks. It was a batch of simple flute-like instruments, obviously handmade.

"Where did you get all those piccolos?" Johnny asked him, wide-eyed with amazement.

"I made them," Joshua answered with a touch of pride in his voice. He had been carving them at odd times over the past week. They were easy to make, once you got the knack of it.

"Gee, they're neat. Do they work?" Johnny persisted, still incredulous.

"Of course they work," Joshua answered with a smile. "Here, Johnny, pass them out."

Johnny took a handful of the little instruments and gave one to each. The kids looked mystified, not knowing what to do with them. One of the boys, Nicholas, began to play his.

"It does work," Johnny said, startled at the happy notes that came out of the little gadget.

Nicholas had a similar instrument at home. His mother, Mary Catherine, had taught him as a young boy how to play it. Soon he was showing the other children how to play theirs. Before long all the children were making sounds, though none could be described as music.

Johnny got an idea when he saw what was taking shape. "Joshua, I have a drum at home. These things would sound great with a drum. Do you want me to go get my drum?"

"Yes, that would be a good idea."

Johnny ran home and was back in no time with the drum strapped over his shoulder, playing little rolls as he walked along. The other children were gradually getting acquainted with their instruments and the sounds were improving. In a little over an hour, with Nicholas guiding them, they were able to play simple melodies and at least have fun together. It was surprising how little it took to whip this little band into a ragtag fife-and-drum corps, not playing perfectly or with any polish, but with good high spirits.

When they had learned to handle the whistles sufficiently, Joshua headed down the road toward the city, with his band of troops behind him. As they walked along a few more children joined. Word of their coming had already preceded them, and as they approached the city, small crowds gathered along the way to greet them, curious to see this strange band of Catholic and Protestant children marching together and making happy music. Everyone was touched. As they passed the people clapped their approval, delighted to see these children playing together but harboring the sad feeling that it would never be allowed to last. There were just too many sick grown-ups who would not take kindly to these children having fun together.

Word had also spread to the fringes of the city that this stranger had managed to attract Catholic and Protestant children into a band of loyal followers who would follow him anywhere, like a modern Pied Piper. It was exciting, particularly in a land where there is little distraction from a monotony of life that can easily evolve into an unrelenting boredom.

On the group went, past the city line and into the city itself, preaching their unspoken message, shocking the whole populace with their bold violation of an ancient taboo that Christians of different labels were forever forbidden to be friends and doomed to permanent enmity. Joshua walked meekly in their midst, proud of these children who had become such loyal friends. The scene was reminiscent of a similar march on a Palm Sunday of so long ago.

By noon the band had reached the park, the same park where Joshua had stopped to listen to the preacher the week before. It was empty now, except for a few old men sitting around smoking their pipes and sharing stories of times gone by. Joshua walked over to the grass and the children followed. Tired, they sat down to rest.

Joshua approached Johnny, who was standing by himself, and quietly spoke to him. "John, the sandwiches you have in your drum, I would like you to quietly share them with the others."

The boy looked up at Joshua mystified and, with an embarrassed smile, asked him, "How did you know I have sandwiches in the drum?"

"John, just go ahead and share," Joshua said gently.

Johnny released the bands holding the drumhead in place and took out one of the two sandwiches and gave it to the boy nearest him. To Johnny's surprise, when he looked back inside the drum there were still two sandwiches. He took another one and gave it to one of the girls near him. Again looking back in the drum, he still saw two sandwiches.

Some of the children noticed the bewildered look on Johnny's face and, out of curiosity, came over to see what was in the drum—two sandwiches. They noticed, however, that as Johnny took out one sandwich after another, there were still two sandwiches left. After he had finished feeding everyone, and even those who wanted seconds, there were still two sandwiches remaining in the drum.

Going over to Joshua, he asked him if he would like a sandwich. "Yes, I would," Joshua replied. "Thank you, John."

"Don't thank me, thank yourself. You're the one who made them."

Joshua smiled, blessed the children, and ate his sandwich. While they were all eating a little girl asked Joshua if he would tell them a story. The children, even the boys, liked Joshua's stories.

"All right. If you gather around me and sit quietly, I'll tell you a story."

The children gathered around in a semicircle on the grass and Joshua began. "A little girl was troubled because she felt she was not pretty and no one liked her. She spent many hours each day by herself, afraid to make friends. Other children were afraid to approach her because she was so quiet. Secretly they admired her because she was kind and never said anything hurtful about anyone. The shy girl watched all the other children laughing and talking and having fun and wanted very much to be part of their life. When she prayed she asked God to help her be happy and make friends. But she never heard God speak to her, not realizing that God does not have to use words to talk to us.

"One day, as the girl was leaving school, she saw a girl whom everyone considered beautiful and who had many friends. The shy girl told her how beautiful she was and how she envied her popularity. The other girl was surprised and confided to her, 'I wasn't always popular. Others thought I was vain and snobbish because I was pretty, and it was very hard for me to make friends. I went out of my way to be kind to others and talk to them even though they didn't seem anxious to talk to me. Gradually I made friends, and if I am popular today, it is because I have tried so hard and for so long to care for others and to make others happy when they are with me. Secretly I always admired you and wanted to be your friend, but I was afraid to talk to you because you are so quiet.'

"The shy girl was surprised and told her, 'I am not really that way. I am afraid of people because I think they are better than I, and I can't see why anyone would like me.'

" 'But we all feel that way,' the other girl said. 'It's part of being human.' That was a shock to the shy girl, who thought she was the only one who felt that way about herself.

"The next day at school the shy girl went out of her way to talk to the other children. She was thrilled to see how quickly they responded, and in a short time she had friends, friends who told her how glad they were she was their friend because so much goodness and joy come into their lives from knowing her.

"The point of the story," Joshua continued, "is very simple. First, God does answer our concerns. He speaks sometimes through things that happen and sometimes through others. On rare occasions he tells us in words or thoughts. The shy girl is like everyone. Every young person feels alone and unworthy. The key to making friends is to care. When we care we touch others' hearts and in our kindness heal their wounds. Kindness is the beginning of friendship."

All during the story the children sat spellbound. The way Joshua taught, the children listened, because it touched their lives. Joshua knew that children hurt just as much as adults, and if religion is to make sense to children, it has to deal with their very real troubles and concerns, not grown-ups' concerns.

When Joshua finished the children clapped. They enjoyed his stories. They were simple, and each one felt he was talking to them personally. And he was. He knew their hearts and knew their hurts. He also had his own understanding of what religion should do for people. It should reconcile people to their Father in heaven and heal wounds in people's hearts and in their lives with one another. Those who aid in that are truly religious. Those who refuse to reconcile and nurse hatreds are the truly evil people.

The picnic over, Joshua led his band of little disciples back home. The walk home wasn't as much fun, nor was the music playing as high-spirited, but each of the children had a chance to talk to Joshua alone as they took turns walking next to him along the way. Each one felt he or she had something special with Joshua, and they felt at ease talking to him about things they would never dare to share with anyone else. Joshua's effect on these children's lives was profound. They were still the same children with the same ways as before, but now they saw things differently and looked at one another differently. They had a vision of how beautiful their lives could be, whereas before their lives were boring and tense. They had been led into a whole new world, one that had always existed but had passed unnoticed.

Back in the village the children thanked Joshua for all the fun they had had and then scattered in all directions. They couldn't wait to tell their families what they had done and show them the piccolos Joshua had made for them.

CHAPTER 18

THE REVEREND DAVIS and Father Donnelly had been trying to track Joshua down all day. The children they had asked to give him a message didn't know where he and the rest of the children had gone. His march to the city had been unannounced. Finally one of the children found Joshua as he was returning from his march.

"Joshua, Joshua," the boy called out to him. "I've been looking all over for you. My pastor, Reverend Davis, wants you to come over to his house tonight for dinner. The priest is coming too. I'm supposed to tell my pastor if you can come."

"Yes," Joshua said, "tell him I will be there. Did he say what time?"

"Five o'clock."

"Tell him I would be happy to come, and thank him, Edward," Joshua said casually.

The boy was startled when Joshua used his name. Even though he had been in the group with Joshua's friends almost every day, he had never spoken to him alone and was surprised he knew his name. The same thing happened to other children, which was another reason they felt so close to him.

It was after three. Joshua walked past the square and

into the meadow toward the brook, his favorite spot, near the tree. There was a cool breeze sweeping across the meadow, a welcome relief from the warm sun that had been beating down on the marchers as they returned from the city.

Joshua sat down under the tree, closed his eyes for a few minutes, and rested before continuing across to a little pond he had discovered farther over in the meadow. It was fed by the brook as it came off the hill. Here Joshua could bathe, fish, and just relax.

At five o'clock Joshua arrived at the manse. Kathie and Meredith answered the door and welcomed him warmly. A few minutes later Father Donnelly arrived. They were both escorted into the pastor's study, a large, warm room with high bookcases lining the walls from ceiling to floor and filled with books, some antique, some quite recent, a few by modern theologians. On the pastor's desk were two books lying open, probably in preparation for next Sunday's sermon. In the center of the room, on a butler's table, was a plate of hors d'oeuvres that Meredith had made and a tray of wine and cocktail glasses. On the wall behind the desk was an old print of John Calvin in a beautifully carved maple frame.

"Joshua, my friend," Father Donnelly said as he entered the room, "I hear you had a busy day. Some of the children told me all about their march on the city. Did you conquer the big, evil Nineveh or was this just the first skirmish?"

Joshua laughed. He knew the priest had him figured out, at least as to his immediate intentions. "No, this was just the first scouting expedition. It went quite well. The children learned to play those little whistles with surprising speed. I guess it was their enthusiasm."

"And no doubt," the priest added, "a touch of magic from yourself. Speaking of magic, by the way, I brought a little rubber ball. I hear you can do marvels with these things."

Joshua laughed heartily. "I see the kids have been telling stories out of school."

At that point the Reverend Davis entered and momentarily interrupted the exchange. He welcomed the two of them, spotted the rubber ball, and quickly sized up the situation. "Oh, I see the word's gotten around about the magic rubber ball."

Father Donnelly picked up where he had left off. "I was just about to see what our magician friend can do with this thing," he said, tossing the ball to Joshua.

Joshua caught it, and as soon as it landed in his hand it disappeared. "I think you're playing tricks on me," Joshua said, looking at the two of them with an impish grin. "How did you do that?" he asked the priest with mock seriousness.

The old priest was mystified, and Joshua did nothing to clear up the mystery. They searched him and looked around the room, on the sofa and chairs, even got down on their hands and knees like two kids and crawled around looking under the furniture.

At that point Kathie walked in, and astonished at seeing the two dignified clerics crawling around on the rug, expressed her disbelief. "My gracious, what on earth are you two doing? How undignified!"

Joshua couldn't restrain his glee and just stood there saying to Kathie, "I can't imagine what's come over them. They seemed quite normal a few minutes ago. Do they always act like that when they get together?"

The two men were thoroughly embarrassed, realizing

how silly they looked, knowing Kathie could in no way understand what they were doing and they could in no way explain. Joshua continued laughing as the two men composed themselves.

"Well, let's get on with the serious business," Rev. Davis said. "I know it's against our rules to have alcoholic beverages, but charity comes before all else, and I know you two could use something refreshing, so what can I serve you? I have almost everything in stock," he said, opening the carefullly concealed panel hiding the liquor closet.

"I know you drink scotch, Elmer," he said to the priest. "Straight or with water?"

"A little bubble water and a little ice will do fine, Russ," the priest answered.

"Joshua, wine or a cocktail?"

Joshua hesitated a moment, then noticing a few bottles of wine, asked, "Do you have sherry?"

"I sure do. I just got it last week, my favorite," he said as he pulled out the cork and poured it carefully into a beautifully cut crystal wineglass. Its deep amber color sparkled in the glass.

Looking at his wife, Russ asked her, "Dear, what would you like?"

"What I usually have, thank you," which meant a tall vodka and tonic.

After serving his wife he poured his own drink, a glass of sherry, commenting, "I realize, gentlemen, this is not in our tradition, but Jesus said if you believe, you can do wonders. If Jesus could change water into wine, then, with faith, there's no reason I can't do the reverse. Though, I have to admit, I've been trying for a long time and it just doesn't seem to work, but I keep trying. I know my parishioners would be horrified."

Russ raised his glass in toast to their friendship and in blessing on Joshua's work with the children, which was the most courageous and noble deed he had ever encountered.

After the toast Kathie lifted the platter of hors d'oeuvres and offered them to the priest. He chose one, and as he raised it to his mouth he found himself about to bite into a rubber ball. Kathie almost dropped the platter in astonishment. Russ saw what had happened and laughed. The old priest, a little embarrassed at first over the unexpected shock, recovered and laughed at Joshua's remarkable sense of humor. The thought flashed across his mind of something Jesus had done two thousand years ago, telling Peter to go fishing and the first fish he catches will have two coins in its mouth, enough to pay the temple tax. From that moment the priest began to wonder.

"See, Kathie," Elmer said, "that's what we were looking for when you came into the room. Joshua made the thing disappear."

Joshua acted as if he had not the slightest idea of what was going on.

The priest put the ball in his pocket, took another hors d'oeuvre, and ate it hurriedly, before something happened to it. He then reached down in his pocket and felt something warm and furry. He tried to act nonchalant as he took the thing out of his pocket. It was a tiny rabbit. Everyone was delighted.

"Now, Elmer," Joshua said, "how did you do that?"

The priest offered the rabbit to Kathie, who politely refused it. Not knowing what to do with it, he put it on the mantel. The ball began to roll along the mantel, so he took it and put it back in his pocket, relieved.

Russ was watching the whole thing, trying to figure out what was happening. He could accept a magician's sleight of hand, but this seemed to go beyond that. What was happening? Joshua, still in the playful vein of having fun, was not about to destroy the illusion, or was it an illusion? He said nothing to clear up the mystery.

Finally relaxing, they all sat down and proceeded to get acquainted. It was really the first time the two clerics had had a chance to talk intimately with Joshua, and there were so many things they were interested in discussing with him.

At first they exchanged pleasantries, and then began to talk about the complicated present-day work of the clergy. It was no longer a simple matter of a nice Sunday service and an interesting Sunday-school program. Now it was the much more serious matter of facing the violent crises in society and helping the people to adjust to very painful and sometimes tragic situations in a way that was Christian. Each of these two men had had tragedies in their congregations. Russ's own brother had been murdered by Catholic fanatics. Elmer's closest friends had been murdered by Protestant extremists. The miracle in the men's lives was that they were still able to love and be Christian.

"I had a man come in the other day," Russ confided. "He told me he hated Catholics. As a child he had seen his grandfather murdered by Catholics and had to live with those terrible memories all his life. Now his daughter tells him she wants to marry a Catholic, and he's torn apart. They had a violent scene in their house the night she broke the news, and he hasn't slept since. He knows I have a reputation for being conciliatory, and he also knows my own personal tragedy and that my mother was a Catholic, but no matter what I said to him, I could not reach him. I didn't sleep well myself that night. Things are so different from what they used to be."

"You're right, Russ," Elmer agreed. "Things used to be so simple. I'm glad I don't have too many years left. My heart's been broken a thousand times with all this senseless tragedy and meanness. I don't think my heart can bear much more pain."

Joshua just listened and felt for these two good men who were trying under the most difficult circumstances to do the right thing and teach others to think straight and to forgive when tragedy struck their families. Both men were trying so hard to be responsive to the Spirit of God, and Joshua could add nothing new to what they already knew, but he felt constrained to offer some hope.

"An end is coming," he said with a finality that hinted of an awareness the others did not share. "It won't be long, and all your efforts will reap their harvest. Don't lose heart. My Father will never let your toil in his vineyard go unrewarded. And it will be a rich harvest. There will be deep hurt and loss, but for only a brief dark day, then a new life for all of you. And you will lead your people together in one family."

"Joshua, you dream," Elmer said.

"No, I speak of what I see and what I see is true, not darkly as in a dream, but clearly as I see it coming to pass in the full light of day. My Father's purpose will not be frustrated nor my mission to bring peace."

"You give me goose bumps when you talk like that," Kathie said to Joshua. "But I do have to admit that, from what I hear, you are surely working wonders with those children. I do hope it lasts."

"Never lose hope. It will happen. My Father's desire is for peace, not destruction. When troubles start do not be afraid and do not judge by appearance. As you have seen before in a playful way, truth is not always what it appears to be," he said with a grin.

The conversation then turned to lighter topics, and before long they were laughing and enjoying the fun of getting to know one another and, for a few brief moments, forgetting all about wars and tragedies. At one point Elmer said to Joshua, "You know, Joshua, you don't come across as a particularly religious person, and yet your attitudes and insights betray a depth of spirituality that could come only from unusual intimacy with God."

Joshua smiled. "I do not attempt to be religious. That has no meaning. To be perfectly human, as God made us, should be our goal. If we appear to be religious or pious, we've missed the point and our piety becomes a caricature and unauthentic. Real holiness is the natural growth of the human personality to its full maturity as an individual, and in the process, becoming a beautiful person. That is all that God wants of us. And since each individual is unique, and has a different task to accomplish in God's plan, each one has to grow differently, so holiness for each individual is different and has nothing to do with predetermined religious patterns and practices that mimic real holiness. Jesus lived in Nazareth for thirty years, and the kids he grew up with were shocked when he began to preach. They never looked upon him as particularly holy, and yet he was the holy one of God."

Now it was Russ's turn. He was concerned about Joshua's long-term plan for the children. "Joshua, if I may run the risk of being presumptuous, what are you trying to accomplish in bringing the children together? You must realize it will never be allowed for very long. Yet, I sense you have already considered that and planned past it. And that precisely is my question. What do you have in mind when people try to stop you?"

Joshua became pensive. "Yes, I have considered the future. Naturally I am concerned, but I trust my Father and it is his will that nothing should happen to the children. What is taking place here will spread, and as it spreads no one can stop it because hatred is paralyzed in the presence of love.

"Adults are sick with hatred and unforgiveness. It is a disease that has no cure, because people who hate need to hate and resist a cure because it means an end to hatred, which they cannot give up. That is why only children can solve the problems you are facing. When children unite in a common goal, the adult world is powerless to stop them. Adults are always at a loss to deal with the innocence of children. I realize you must all be concerned about what I am doing, but do not be afraid. It is the only way."

"Joshua, you talk about 'my father.' What do you mean when you say that?" Russ asked delicately.

"God is my Father and your Father," he replied. "I could have said 'our Father,' but it is not the way we speak. I have always done the will of my Father, and I understand his ways and how events unfold. That is why I am not afraid for the children."

With all the talk, Kathie had a difficult time tearing the men away for supper. She had outdone herself in preparing the meal and couldn't wait to serve it: a rack of lamb, an array of tastefully prepared potatoes and vegetables, and an imported wine, which Joshua thought almost as good as the wine at Cana, but not quite as delicately aged.

The whole evening turned out to be a warm and comforting experience. The three found their guest to be an extraordinary man, so casually simple, but with an uncanny knowledge of events and people, which caused them to wonder about how such a simple and unassuming person could come upon such immense understanding. And all during the evening they felt a peaceful joy unlike anything they had ever experienced.

Before long it was time for the old priest to go home. They agreed to get together again sometime very soon. Russ and Kathie insisted Joshua stay at their house for the night. Somehow it did not seem right to just send him off to sleep in the meadow, so Joshua spent the night there in a warm bed for a change.

CHAPTER 19

WORD about Joshua's march to the city spread far. It wasn't just children who were fascinated. Grown-ups were interested, some out of curiosity, others for more obscure reasons, concerned no doubt about the long-term implications of something like this turning into a crusade. News reporters and other media people had heard about the march and were asking questions about this man Joshua whom everyone was talking about. Who was he? Where did he live? How do we contact him? Actually, Joshua would have been the last one to call his little hike a march. That had too many political implications, and Joshua was not political. He was concerned only that people care for one another and learn to live in peace as God's children.

Rev. Davis had gotten a phone call earlier that day from a reporter with the *Evening News* inquiring about Joshua. Russ told him what Joshua was doing, how he lived, what he thought of his attempts to unite the children, and the very favorable reactions of the adults in the area. When asked how he could contact this man, Russ told him he could come down and see for himself and get the story live. "He is around most all the time, if you really want to talk with him," he ended up telling him.

Joshua was in the square with the children, talking to

Joe about his trumpet lesson, when the reporter arrived. The newsman parked his car off to the side of the square and stood on the side just watching and taking notes. Joshua noticed, and for a brief moment the thought flashed across his memory of long ago when others used to take notes of everything he said and did. But this man was different. They didn't have newspapers or reporters in those days. This man could be an asset—in fact, a valuable means of accomplishing almost overnight what would take him by himself many months of hard work and travel.

Joe let Joshua practice for a few minutes. He had made remarkable progress since his first lesson and it was beginning to show. He could now play tunes that were a little less simple than the ones he first learned, and the children were impressed. Exercising his lip was a problem because Joshua never really practiced, and without practice there is no way to strengthen your lip to play the instrument with any degree of proficiency. What he did play was exciting enough for the children and that was all Joshua cared about. He had no illusions about becoming a concert artist.

The reporter watched Joshua with interest—how he noticed every child, letting nothing escape his eye, making sure each one received attention, and the personal way he treated each one. It was a lesson in psychology, and it was no longer just little children who were in the group. There were a number of older kids well into their teens for whom Joshua was obviously their hero. There was also a new boy who had come for the first time. He was different from the others, standing out because of his dark features and jet-black hair. A boy about twelve was leading him by the hand. On closer look you could see that the dark boy was blind. The two of them were standing near Joshua, who noticed them but said nothing.

After Joshua played the trumpet for a few minutes, he gave the instrument back to Joe and asked him to play for the children. He did. The contrast was dramatic. It was obvious that Joshua was no trumpet player. Joe's playing was superb. Even though a child, his mastery of the high notes and the trills was remarkable for a boy of his age. The children loved to hear him play. It was a high point of their get-togethers, and even Joshua enjoyed the boy's mastery of the instrument. What was beautiful, though, was the humility of Joshua. It was of no concern that a little boy could outshine him in front of all the others.

The routine this day was the same as every other day. The little personal engagements with various children, the entertainment, the storytelling, and Joshua talking individually with children who had things they wanted to share with him. The reporter stayed to watch the whole routine, and when most of the children had left, he walked over to Joshua and waited politely as he talked to the little blind boy and his friend. The two children looked toward the reporter, then stepped to the side, as if Joshua had told them to wait until the man left.

"My name is Brad Broyles," the man said, introducing himself to Joshua. "I'm a reporter for the *Evening News*. I must admit I am fascinated by the influence you obviously have on these children. Would you mind if I interview you?"

"Not at all," Joshua said graciously.

"How long have you lived here in the village?"

"Just a few weeks."

"Where are you from?"

"I travel here and there."

"What brought you to the village?"

"The thought of helping the good people here to find peace."

"Do you think you can do anything about it?"

"Yes, otherwise I wouldn't be here."

"Why spend all your time with the children when it's the adults who have the problem?"

"Because adults resist change, and once adults learn to hate, it is hard for them to forgive and lay aside their hatred. Children are the only hope of the future. If they can learn to love one another before they are taught to hate, then they will be able to grow up together as friends, and as friends there are no problems that cannot be solved."

"How do you intend to go about this?"

"As you have seen. Children like to see a world at peace, and they like to be friends with neighbors. It makes them feel secure and at peace themselves. You can see how well they get along, and it will spread."

"Do you think people are going to be happy with what you are doing?"

"It is clear many people already are pleased enough to let their children come each day."

"But there are others . . ." the reporter went on to say without finishing.

"There will always be 'others.' That will have to be their problem. The overriding interest of God is not perfect happiness or perfectly just societies in this world. It was not a just or perfect society in Jesus' day, and yet he was interested not in revolutions to resolve that problem, but in people focusing their vision on God and finding peace within themselves. If that message had spread, there would be just societies today. Turmoil in society is the expression of the torture within individuals. But few of his followers have ever taken Jesus seriously, so you still have a sick world, with his followers destroying one another. It is a scandal to unbelievers. That is God's real concern, the damage done to his creation by those who profess his name. And their wanton destruction of his children will not go unpunished."

Not getting caught up in the heat of Joshua's concern, the reporter continued, "But aren't you concerned precisely because of that?"

"My vision of the future is clear, and I am not concerned. I know what my Father has in store, and his intention is peace."

"Who is your father? You talk as if he is a politician."

"He is my Father and your Father. The world is his, and he cares for his children."

The reporter was unaccustomed to hearing people speak this way and was beginning to feel uneasy, but he still continued with his line of questioning. "How do the clergy accept what you are doing?"

"They have been supportive, as you already know," which unsettled the reporter, who was wondering how Joshua knew he had talked to the clergy.

The interview lasted a few minutes longer, after which the reporter thanked Joshua and left, but not before he interviewed the two children.

"What is your name?" he asked the blind boy.

"Acmet," he answered.

"That's a different kind of name. What nationality are you?"

"I am Arab," the boy answered simply.

"Do you live here?"

"Yes, I have lived here all my life."

"How old are you?"

"Nine."

"What happened to your eyes?" the reporter asked without any feeling.

"I had an accident and hit my head, but I am getting better," the boy said with a trace of fright in his voice.

"Do you like Joshua?" the reporter then asked.

"Yes, I do."

And the other boy added, "We all do."

"What is your name, sonny?"

"My name is Peter."

"How long have you known Joshua?"

"Since he came here. I met him the second day."

"Why does everyone like him so much?"

"Because he makes us feel good inside and happy, and he is kind and teaches us how to be friends."

"Is Acmet your friend?"

"Yes, we are good friends. I brought him to see Joshua because I thought Joshua might pray for him and make him see."

"Does he do things like that?"

"I don't know, but he healed a friend of mind whose arm was blown off by a hand grenade."

Joshua, in the meantime, had distanced himself from the three, anticipating what the children might say, and was too far away when the reporter turned to verify the story.

The reporter, having all the information he needed, thanked the children and left. Peter took Acmet by the hand and led him across the square to find Joshua. He was sitting on a rock at the edge of the meadow.

"Joshua," Peter said, "the reporter asked us questions. Do you think we will be in the newspaper?"

"Yes, I am sure you will."

"I can't wait to read it," Peter responded, to which Acmet agreed.

"Joshua, could you bless Acmet and make him see?" Peter asked hopefully.

Joshua said nothing, just thought for what seemed a very long time. Peter looked at him imploringly.

"Acmet, do you want to see?" Joshua asked the boy.

"Yes, I do, very much."

"Do you believe I can heal you?" he continued.

"Yes, Joshua, because you are a good man, and my parents said you are close to God. I know God will listen to you if you ask him. Please, Joshua, I want so much to be able to see again."

Joshua looked at the boy.

"Come here, Acmet," Joshua said.

Peter led his friend to Joshua's side. Joshua rested his hands on the boy's head, and with his thumbs touched his eyes. The boy stepped back and opened them, and his face began to glow with excitement and joy. "I can see, I can see," he screamed with delight. Turning toward Peter, he hugged him and cried with happiness.

Peter walked over to Joshua. With a happy smile he put out his hand and, in a very boyish, businesslike way, shook Joshua's hand, thanking him for healing his friend. "Joshua, I knew you would be able to heal him. You are always so kind to everyone. You are my best friend. Thank you."

"Yes, Joshua, thank you so much for helping me see," the little Arab boy said as he hugged Joshua. "I will never forget you."

The two boys ran off across the square, hopping with a joy they had never known, unable to wait to tell their families what had happened. Joshua watched them, smiling, then walked into the meadow.

20

Joshua spent the rest of the afternoon at the coast, sitting on the rocks and meditating. God had programmed tranquilizers into nature, and Joshua knew how to draw serenity and calm from his Father's presence in His creation. It was just as important for him to take time alone as it was for him to be busy at his work. Indeed, it seemed to be the source of the remarkable orderliness and purpose that pervaded his whole life.

Meanwhile, the reporter had gone back to the office to write up his story and told his editor he expected something big to break eventually with this man Joshua because the political implications of what he was doing were just too explosive. In fact, various individuals in the city were already discussing Joshua's activities and assessing his motives. The pubs were beginning to hum with snide remarks about this fellow who had all the kids following him. Acmet and Peter had run home to tell their story. Acmet's parents were beside themselves with happiness and immediately set about discussing how to show their appreciation to Joshua for having healed their son. They asked the children where Joshua lived. They didn't know. They thought he might just live in the fields, because that's where he always seemed to be. Peter offered to look for him. Miriam, Acmet's mother, told him if he found

Joshua to ask if he would honor them by coming to their home so they could thank him properly for what he had done for their son. This was remarkable. Joshua was not used to being thanked. It was also true of long ago. Only one example, and that was a stranger.

Peter set out, running down the street. There was no need to run, but the little fellow was that way, high-spirited and brimming over with life, never content for things to happen slowly, always trying to rush time so things would happen faster. Down across the square, along the path into the meadow, and to the pond, where he knew Joshua went sometimes. He was not there, but three kids were swimming. He asked them if they had seen Joshua. Yes, they had. He had passed by the pond a while ago and said he was on his way to the seashore.

Peter was crestfallen and disappointed, but, undaunted, he rested with the kids for a few minutes and then took off for the coast. He found Joshua sitting on a boulder just watching the water crashing up against the rocks beneath. He watched him for a few minutes, wondering why he came out here all alone, then walked out along the rocks to deliver his message.

"Joshua," Peter called. The roar of the water was overpowering. He called a second time. Joshua turned around and saw the little boy standing on the rocks not far behind him.

"Peter," he said, surprised, "what are you doing way out here?"

"I've come to deliver a message. Acmet's parents want you to come to their house so they can thank you for healing Acmet." He got it all out in almost one breath.

Joshua smiled. "They don't have to thank me," he said.

"I know, but they want to."

"Well, come over here and sit down and we will talk about it."

Peter jumped over the rocks and came to where Joshua was. He sat down on the rock next to him.

"Isn't the sea beautiful, Peter?" Joshua said to the boy.

"Yes, I've been out here before, once when I was a little boy. We came here for a picnic," Peter responded. "I come here with my friends sometimes."

"You can feel God's presence resting above the water. The sea looks so lifeless, but it is teeming with life. There are more living things in the ocean waters than there are in all the land. People don't understand the ocean and how important it is for them. The future of human life on earth is in the vast ocean waters. They should be protected and kept pure and not used as a dump.

"I notice, Peter, that you are a very happy boy. You enjoy life, don't you?"

"Yes, but doesn't everybody?"

"Not really. There are many who are sad and many who are angry, and they don't know how to enjoy life. You are a rare happy person, like that swallow flying above the rocks over on the cliff," he said as he watched the swallow darting about in the water spray around the rocks.

"There was once a little boy very much like you. He liked to play and to have fun, and he brought happiness to everyone. God created him for a very special work and tried to send messages to this little boy so He could guide him, but the messages were never received because the boy was too busy to hear God's quiet voice. The boy grew up and went from job to job, not happy with his life. All his happy ways disappeared. One day he decided to take a walk into a quiet meadow just to think. He didn't even intend to pray. He had long ago stopped that. While he walked he felt the presence of God, and in his heart God talked to him, and the boy finally listened. From that day on his life changed. He had found his friendship with God, and God was able to use him to do beautiful things with his life. It is so important to take time to listen to the gentle voice of God. That is the way he guides you."

"Is that what you are doing here, Joshua?" the boy asked innocently.

"Yes. I enjoy coming into the presence of God. He guides me. He teaches me. He brings me peace. And I always walk away with joy in my heart. God made us to be his friends, not to walk alone.

"Let's get up and walk back home," Joshua said, rising from the rock where he had been sitting.

The two walked back across the fields and over the hills. As they approached the village Peter told Joshua he was going ahead to tell Acmet's family that he would come to visit them. "What time do you think you will be there, so I can tell them?" he said, trying to pin Joshua down.

"I will stop over later this evening, around eight. And thank you, Peter, for going all the way out there to give me that message."

"That's okay. I was glad to because I got a chance to talk with you. You're my friend, and I like being with you," the boy replied as he ran off.

21

JOSHUA had wanted to stop off at Tommy and Millie's house. He knew Tommy had been ill and was concerned for the couple. Life was not easy for the elderly couple and Millie wasn't up to caring for the farm herself. It was a frightening experience when one of them got sick.

Millie was surprised to see Joshua when she answered the door. She had just finished working in the barn and was busy getting things ready for supper.

"Oh, young man, I'm afraid you've come at a bad time. Tom is in bed sick, and I am running myself ragged trying to get things done around here. I can't even offer you a decent bite to eat. Though you're welcome to stay for supper if you like."

"No, Millie. Thank you for your kindness. I just wanted to visit with Tom for a minute. I heard he was sick."

"How did you know? I haven't told anyone, and there's not a soul who knows it," she said, bewildered.

"I just knew, Millie, and was concerned. I can't stay long."

"The ol' goat is in the bedroom," she said in feigned toughness. "Go right in. He'll be glad to see you."

It was a simple bedroom, with a wooden chair, a

dresser, and a large bed filling most of the small room. On the walls were pictures of old folks, no doubt Tom and Millie's parents, and assorted relatives.

Tom brightened up when Joshua came in, really surprised to see him. He looked weak and drawn as he tried to gesture for Joshua to take the chair and sit down.

Joshua walked over to the bed and grasped the old man's hands in his own, telling him he was sorry that he was ill. Tom was just as shocked as Millie was to find that Joshua knew. Joshua wouldn't give him any more satisfaction than he gave his wife, and Tom didn't pursue it.

"Sit down there, young man," he said to Joshua. "It was real nice of you to come visit me. I sometimes feel I'm at the end of the line. I feel so weak. When I get sick like this I worry so much about my wife. Life is hard here, and I know she won't be able to take care of everything herself."

"Don't you worry about things like that. That's God's business. You just do your work and enjoy the time God gives you. Worry has never changed a thing. Trust God. He watches over you like a mother hen," Joshua said, attempting to reassure the old man.

"The doctor was out earlier today and said there isn't anything he can do for me. Told me just to rest and not get excited and make sure I stay in bed. My heart is worn out, I guess."

Millie came into the room with a cup of tea and a little dish full of cookies and placed them on the dresser next to Joshua.

"Thank you, Millie," Joshua said appreciatively.

The three of them talked for a few minutes, then Joshua got up to go. Before leaving he walked close to the bed and, reaching down, rested his hand on Tom's head and caressed the side of his face, telling him quietly, "Tom, be at peace. God has answered your prayers. You are well again."

The couple listened, not understanding. Tom felt what Joshua had said. He knew he was well again. A bit carefully at first, then spryly, he jumped out of the bed, and with tears flowing down his cheeks, he grabbed Joshua's hand and thanked him, then hugged his wife.

"Keep this to yourself," Joshua told them. "I don't want this to get around. It will complicate my work and create too much confusion." They were both quiet people and had no intention of telling anyone, though they treasured the experience in their hearts.

As Joshua was leaving the couple walked him to the door. Tom, in his nightshirt, stood on the porch waving to him like a little child as Joshua walked across the barnyard toward the road.

Joshua continued down the road toward the village, and crossing the square, he walked down into the Catholic side of town, the area where the Arab family lived. Peter had not told Joshua where his friends lived, and when the family realized that they wondered if Joshua would find them. Like many other unexplained things, Joshua knew.

He knocked at their door. The little boy answered, expecting Joshua's coming. He was wide-eyed with excitement when he saw who it was, and forgetting to invite him inside, Acmet ran into the house screaming, "It's Joshua, it's Joshua. He's here."

His parents, trying to act calm, walked out into the foyer and were embarrassed to see Joshua still standing outside. "Our sincerest apologies for our son not inviting you into our home," Acmet's father said. "He has been waiting all day for you to come and is so excited he can't contain himself."

"I understand. I am delighted by his childlike enthusiasm. It shows such simple innocence," Joshua replied.

"Please come in. I am Acmet's father. My name is Anwar, and this is my wife, Miriam. Our home is your home, as humble as it is. We are honored that you have come. It was presumptuous of us to invite you. We should have come to you, but we didn't know where you live and we wanted so much to be able to thank you properly for the wonderful thing you have done for our son. Please make yourself at home." The man guided Joshua to the living room. The house was unusually large by local standards, fashioned more after well-to-do people's homes of the Mideast rather than conventional homes of the area. There were Persian rugs scattered in all the rooms. The living room had a large fireplace and oriental antiques were placed discreetly around the room. The furniture was elegant French Provincial. Joshua looked very ordinary in such an opulent setting, and yet, at this point, he, and not the family's wealth, was the cause for all their happiness.

As soon as Joshua was seated the mother asked politely if Joshua had had supper. She asked in such a way that it was clear she hoped he had not and was delighted when he said he would stay. The father offered him a glass of wine, which Joshua accepted. After a few minutes everyone seemed more relaxed and Joshua seemed very much at home. That put the family at ease. It is so comfortable being in the presence of this gentle man, they thought, and yet there was much more to him than appeared on the surface. They could see an innate nobility and dignity about Joshua that belied the ordinariness of his dress.

What a beautiful man! Joshua sat in his chair with an air that hinted royalty, yet it wasn't contrived. It was just his way. Even dressed in his poor attire, his natural dignity radiated. They were so honored to have this man in their home.

As they sipped wine the father asked Joshua about himself, and he could see that Joshua was more than just a run-of-the-mill Christian. "Joshua, my son has been talking about you ever since Peter introduced him to you. The children tell us all the stories. I just listen and develop my own ideas. From what the children say, if it is true, you are not an ordinary man. I have read the Gospels and I can see such precise similarities between the things that you do and say and what Jesus did and said that I can't help but feel . . . I won't have the presumption to ask, but your healing my son convinced me. Joshua, I want to let you know that my life and my family are at your service. Whatever we can do for you, we would be honored if you ask."

"Anwar," Joshua responded, "you are not far from the kingdom of God. The lights you have are not your own. It is my Father who has given light to your mind. You will honor me by following where God leads you. His Son is the Gate of Heaven, the Door to Salvation. Do not be afraid to follow where he leads. God's way is not a way of violence but a way of peace that he wants for his children. Those who honor that peace are truly God's children."

Anwar flushed with embarrassment, realizing Joshua knew of his family's clandestine arms shipments to terrorists. Meeting Joshua, he now saw everything clearly and in different focus, and he meant to reassure Joshua that things were no longer the same. "Joshua, I regret what has happened in the past. I felt, as did my family, that what we were doing was helping suppressed people, out of a feeling of solidarity, but I can now see destroying God's children is not the path that is pleasing to God. I assure you that things will be different. We will continue in our own way and with our abundant resources to work for justice for our neighbors. They are good people and have suffered much, just like our own people back home."

"Anwar, it is a noble work to sacrifice for justice. God did not intend to finish his creation. Much has been left undone, so men and women can fulfill their purpose on earth by channeling God's riches to one another. Hunger, poverty, and injustice exist because so many horde God's treasures for themselves and their families, or for political power, and the rest of the world goes starving or in dire want. It is not the will of God. It is the sin of those who refuse to share what God has entrusted to them. It is for such that hell exists, for they will be unable to bear the reflection of their own greed and selfishness in the face of God's infinite goodness and out of shame will forever choose to hide from God's love, preferring the company of those like themselves, totally self-centered and devoid of love."

Miriam interrupted to bring everyone into the dining room, which was adjacent to the living room and was spacious and richly adorned. Other family members appeared from all over, and by the time supper was served there were over twelve people in all, including some older relatives. Acmet asked if he could sit near Joshua. He was allowed. A whole array of imported Eastern foods was served, all of which Joshua enjoyed, feeling very much at home.

It was a new experience for Joshua to eat at the home of a Muslim family. The evening went well. Joshua heartily enjoyed the warm hospitality of this very grateful and gracious family. As the evening drew on and Joshua made as if to leave, the family insisted he stay, knowing, as everyone else did, that he had no place to call home. They provided a simple but nicely decorated guest room for him, and then, after sitting around talking until far into the evening, they all retired for the night.

22

JOSHUA'S BREAKFAST at the Muslim family's home was reminiscent of breakfasts long past. The family was reluctant to see Joshua leave but were grateful that he would grace their home with his presence. When he was leaving Anwar slipped a small envelope into Joshua's pocket. Catholic people in the neighborhood were surprised to see Joshua leaving a Muslim home. The family was not looked upon kindly by most Catholics, who knew the nature of their political activities and the types of people who collaborated with them. They certainly knew Joshua had no sympathy for what they were doing, and after carefully considering it, surmised his visit had to do with Acmet's sudden healing, which the whole neighborhood knew about.

Jesus once made the remark "Be as simple as a dove, but as sly as a fox." Joshua lived that to perfection. There was a simplicity to everything he did. His purpose was pure and uncomplicated, but he was totally aware of the implications of even his simplest actions as he carefully plotted every little detail of the drama he was orchestrating. It gave one, if he or she chose to look, and if indeed they had the ability to understand, a rare glimpse into the beautiful way God's providence interacts with people's predictable use of their freedom to make decisions.

Joshua's mastery of human psychology made it possible for him to predict reactions to everything he did; he could plan on those reactions to further organize his strategy. He knew precisely what would result from the newspaper story that would be coming out that evening. He would just wait calmly until it unfolded.

As he walked into the square Jane was just starting to feed the birds. The cardinal lately had even been coming closer, though not like when Joshua was there to call him.

"Joshua," she said to him as he approached, "I heard what you did for Acmet yesterday. That was nice of you to be so kind." She didn't fully realize just what he had done for the boy.

Joshua smiled and thanked her. "How are all your little friends this morning? There are more than usual."

"I noticed, and I'm going to have to get more food for them," she replied.

"Don't be concerned, little one," Joshua reassured her, "there is plenty of food for them in the fields. They know you like them. They don't need for you to give them a lot."

Joshua sat down on the stone wall. Jane came and sat next to him. "Joshua," she began by saying, "I heard my father and mother talking. They said you are a strange man, but a good man. They are happy at what you do for us kids, but they are afraid for you. Why are they afraid, Joshua?"

"Don't you trouble yourself about things like that, little one," he answered calmly. "Little children should be happy and not be burdened with troubles that give grown-ups heavy hearts. Enjoy being a child. Don't you worry yourself about Joshua. He is carefully protected in God's heart and no harm will touch him. Joshua is like a beam of light that comes from God to touch your lives and teach you love. Only for a moment will that light seem to go out, but do not be afraid. God will always be near."

The girl was reassured, understanding not a word of what he had said.

Children were entering the square, some coming from Stonecastle Road, others from the opposite direction, casually meeting in the center and greeting each other, no longer carefully but openheartedly, glad to be friends. There weren't many this morning. As Joshua found out, most of the children were going to the city with their parents to shop and to attend a local fair that took place each year at this time. Joe had to play at the fair and his friends went with him and his parents. The ones who came to visit with Joshua were older children, happy that the little kids were not around.

"Joshua, we heard what you did for the little Arab boy. How did you do that?" one of the boys asked.

"You have to realize that God is real," Joshua answered, "and he does care for all of you. When you understand that and let God into your life, you establish a bond between yourself and God. Your faith then can work wonders because the power of God moves freely through your life."

One of the other boys, a Protestant by the name of Robert, told Joshua his father was a politician in the city, that he didn't like what Joshua was doing and didn't want his son associating with him. The boy told his father that Joshua was a good man and he had no intention of not seeing him. A serious disagreement followed and the father stormed out of the house in the middle of supper and didn't come home until after midnight.

"Robert," Joshua responded in a casual, matter-of-fact tone of voice, "children should listen with respect to what parents say, but sometimes parents are more concerned with interests opposed to God's wishes. In those rare instances children must be willing to follow where God leads, even if it means upsetting parents."

"We all know," the boy continued, "that what you are doing is a good thing. The grown-ups here are really sick, and they won't let us live in peace. We have no quarrel with Catholic kids. They are just like us in many ways. You have taught us that and you have taught us to like one another. It is only our parents who don't want us to associate because it will get in the way of their own sick feuds."

Joshua listened attentively, then told the boy he had a great deal of courage and principle and should always follow his conscience.

The children didn't stay with Joshua very long that day. Sometimes just a few minutes to talk about things that troubled them was all they needed, then they would walk away at peace.

Joshua later found the little envelope the Muslim family had given him. It contained a short note thanking him again and telling him they realize he doesn't have much to live on, that they would be happy if he would accept this little token. Inside the note was a hundred-dollar bill. Joshua decided to eat at the tavern that evening. As it was still a few hours until suppertime, he walked up Stonecastle Road and wandered around the Protestant area. It was the nicer part of town. The houses were well kept, the streets nicely cared for, and the atmosphere tranquil. It was a pleasant place to live or even just to walk through.

He came across a blacksmith shop with an old, weather-beaten sign hanging over the doorway inscribed with the words "Charlie's Place." Joshua was curious. He stopped to watch Charlie working around the forge, fabricating things that might be needed on a farm or around the fireplace of an old cottage. The man, gruff but friendly, was well into his sixties.

"What's your name, young man?" he asked Joshua.

"Joshua. I guess you're Charlie."

"Yeah, that's me. And I guess you're the new fellow everyone's talking about. It's a nice thing you're doing with the kids. Wish you a lot of luck."

"Thank you, but that won't be necessary. It will work the way it's planned. I'm fascinated with your work. You really know your trade," Joshua commented.

I should. I've been doing this since I could crawl. I get tired lately. I have orders to get out today and don't have the energy to do this hard work anymore. Haven't been feeling well the past few days."

"Can I help? I'd like to if you'd let me. I used to do this kind of work and really enjoyed it."

The man was surprised at Joshua's pluckiness and immediately took to this friendly stranger. "Yeah, you sure can if you really know how. I could use a few minutes rest. You really think you can handle this thing?" he said, looking at the chain on the forge.

"Yes, I've done it before," Joshua answered as he proceeded to put on the thick leather apron hanging on the wall. In a few minutes he was handling the forge, the tongs, and the hammer and anvil as a professional, and starting to sweat just like a professional. The blacksmith admired his ease in handling the tools.

"You really do know how to handle those things," the man said to Joshua, surprised. "Wouldn't mind having you work for me. I could use some help the next few weeks. I got behind when I started feeling under the weather."

"I'd like to give you a hand," Joshua said, then continued, "but it will only be for the next few weeks."

"Suits me fine," Charlie said, more than happy to accommodate his new helper.

Joshua worked at the forge for almost two hours, then took off the apron and walked to the sink, cupped his hands under the running water, splashed his sweating face, and dried himself with the towel hanging on the wall.

"If you're serious about helping me, I'd appreciate your coming around the same time tomorrow, maybe an hour earlier. That's about the time I run out of steam."

"I'll be here," Joshua said, like a young kid who had just landed his first job. He left the shop happy and walked down the street.

It was about six-thirty when Joshua entered the tavern. The bar was full, with ten or twelve men sitting around busily engaged in light chatter. No one paid much attention to Joshua. Tim McGirr was there but was busy and didn't notice his friend come in. The tavern was a quaint, nostalgic place, with pictures of famous and not-so-famous frequenters from the past. There were about a dozen and a half tables, neatly covered with green-and-white checkered tablecloths, arranged to the right of the bar and spreading down to the back of the room, where there was an open area reserved for any who liked to dance. The bar was ornately carved and looked as if it had been there for centuries. It probably had been. There were a few guests already seated, enjoying the ritual of eating out with friends.

A waiter came over and asked Joshua where he would

like to sit. He said he preferred to sit near the window, so the man led him over to a table far enough away from the bar so that he could have some privacy and also a view of the square. Joshua seemed satisfied.

"Would you like something to drink before supper?" the waiter asked.

"Yes, I would like a glass of sherry, dry," Joshua answered.

"Any particular brand, sir?"

"No, whatever you think is a good one. I'll trust your judgment."

Joshua sat and looked out the window. The square was quiet this time of evening. The declining sun painted soft shadows across the stone pavement. It reminded him of the square at Nazareth, except there was no fountain here where women could come to draw water and share news.

The waiter returned with Joshua's drink and a plate of crackers and cheese. Joshua spread his napkin, lifted his glass, and sipped the wine. He savored the first sip, enjoying its full flavor and bouquet, while the waiter prepared to take Joshua's order.

"What would you like for supper, sir?" he asked.

"I think I'll have ham steak, potatoes, and cabbage."

"And for dessert?"

"A piece of apple pie and a cup of coffee."

"Thank you. It should be ready in a few minutes."

Joshua sat looking out the window, lost in his thoughts as he sipped the wine, every now and then nibbling on the cheese and crackers. A boy came in and dropped off a few newspapers, which immediately circulated among the men at the bar, the bartender quickly grabbing one for himself. In no time the conversation switched to that stranger, Joshua. To their surprise there was an article about him in the paper. "Hey, look at this, guys, there's a story here about the village. It's got a picture of that stranger that hangs around with the kids and a long article."

"Read it!" one of the fellows yelled out.

"Hell, I'm not gonna read that thing in here. I can hardly see straight as it is."

The men started reading over each other's shoulders, and in no time the whole conversation at the bar centered on Joshua. Some were saying he was a good man, well-intentioned but a dreamer. Others said he had to be odd hanging around kids. One fellow, by the name of Matt, who had already had too much to drink, made the remark that he thought Joshua was a troublemaker and should keep the hell out of their affairs. "It's obvious what he's trying to do. He's out to screw up the whole works around here and undermine our cause. I think we should teach the bloody bastard a good lesson."

At that point Tim didn't like the way the dialogue was going so he added his comments. "You guys don't know what you're talking about. He's a decent chap. I had him over to our house one night and we had a long talk. The man's got one hell of a lot of courage if you ask me. It is obvious what he's up to, and I for one am glad. None of us has the guts to do what he's doing. I think the guy's a saint, and anyone who dares to lay a finger on him, I personally will break his bloody jaw. And that goes for you, too, Matt. You and your crew have caused enough trouble around here, and though no one will tell you to your face, we're all fed up with it."

Well, that did it. Tim, who had also put away a few, had crossed the line of barroom etiquette. Matt wasn't going to take that one sitting down, so, sliding off the barstool, he hauled off, catching Tim with a right to the face. Tim's mouth started to bleed. He flushed with anger. Tim hadn't been in a good fight in years, and this one seemed worth it. Joshua was such a decent guy, he was worth fighting for, so he swung and caught Matt on the jaw with an uppercut that sent him sprawling flat on the floor, half unconscious. The others were disappointed it had ended so soon. They had expected a little more excitement than that.

Joshua saw what had happened, and when Matt fell on the floor he went over and helped him up. Matt was ready to go after Tim again, but was shocked to see who it was helping him. Tim was just as shocked. Everyone was a bit embarrassed but invited Joshua to sit at the bar with them. He did.

"Joshua," Tim said, half proud of himself and half ashamed, "you're my friend, and I won't tolerate anyone attacking you."

"I appreciate that, Tim. Peter was that way a long time ago, and all it did was get everyone into trouble. There's nothing so bad it can't be discussed intelligently. And this is not the place to discuss serious issues. It is bound to end up in a fight."

One of the men shoved the newspaper in front of Joshua.

"See the article about you?" he said.

Joshua looked it over, but wasn't very interested. After glancing at it briefly he went back to talking with the men. "Matt is right," Joshua said, to everyone's dismay. Matt beamed. Joshua continued, "I am very concerned about the children. They are your children. You should be concerned about them too. It is cruel and callous to strip the joy out of little children's lives and instill hatred in their hearts that will fester till the day they die. If an evil person wants to destroy a child, the quickest and most vicious way of doing it is to teach that child to hate and to go through life suspicious of others. And here the terrible thing is that parents are doing that to their own children. I have come here to reverse that once and for all. I have come to free the children from hatred and teach them to love. I know full well where it leads, and I am not afraid. But I warn you solemnly, do not interfere with the work of God. You pride yourselves on being religious people. Truly religious people don't do the things that are done here in the name of religion. That blasphemes the name of God, just like others blaspheme the name of God by teaching their followers to hate others of God's children. It is sickness like this that poisons the world and makes peace impossible. Peace cannot exist as long as people enjoy hating. Hatred can end only when individuals choose not to take offense, can overlook the meanness and limitations of others, and understand the troubles that give rise to mean things. Few people grow to be that big."

Even though they were all half drunk, the men were touched by what Joshua said. They could see the goodness in the man's heart and had never heard anyone talk like that before. A couple of the men had tears in their eyes and were trying to hide them, embarrassed that they should become so emotional, though it was partly the effect of the alcohol. Matt had very mixed feelings. He could see the sincerity of Joshua, but, being involved himself, he couldn't justify what Joshua was doing.

The waiter came out with Joshua's supper and asked where he wanted to eat it. The men persuaded Joshua to eat at the bar and talk to them, and that's what he did.

While Joshua ate his supper the men questioned him about everything everyone else had questioned him about.

Joshua answered the same as he had for the others. His answers made sense. Some liked what he had to say and liked what he was doing. Some disagreed. All were concerned about the final outcome, now more than ever since the newspaper had made it a public issue and the idea was bound to spread.

When Joshua finished his drink the men ordered another for him, but he declined graciously. "I enjoyed the one I had, any more wouldn't be the same." The men respected his wishes. They were enjoying this fascinating man. He was serious, but in a lighthearted, playful way that kept the mood light under circumstances that could have become heavy and argumentative.

One by one the men began to leave. Their families were patiently waiting for them to come home for dinner. Before long Joshua was left there with Tim and a couple of Tim's friends. They stayed until Joshua finished eating, then left with him.

"You know you're always welcome at our house for supper," Tim said to Joshua. "You don't have to stand on ceremony. Just pop in anytime. We would be delighted to have you."

"I know, Tim, and I do feel welcome," Joshua responded.

The men parted, going their separate ways. Joshua and Tim walked across the meadow together, Tim pressing Joshua to spend the night at the house.

CHAPTER 23

I<small>T WAS</small> early in the morning when Joshua came into the village. He headed straight for Father Donnelly's place, greeting people along the way. Everyone in town knew him by now. Some made comments about the article in the paper. Joshua just smiled and thanked them, continuing on his way.

The old priest had just finished Mass and was walking out of the church when Joshua came up the walk.

"Good morning, Father," he said with a respect for the venerable priest's age.

"Good morning, son," the priest returned. "I see you're a celebrity. That was quite an article they wrote about you in the paper. I read it with interest. I was surprised they were so sympathetic. Usually they're critical of everything, but they must have liked you to write the way they did. It will surely give a good push to what you're trying to do. Can you come in for a few minutes?"

"Yes, if you're not busy," Joshua answered.

"Not at all. Come right in," the priest said, ushering his friend into the parish house.

Marie was inside getting breakfast ready. She was glad to see Joshua and greeted him warmly. The two men sat down at the table in the dining room. It was small compared to the one at the manse, but the priest ate alone most of the time and didn't need anything spacious. There was a picture of the Pope on the wall and a smaller photo portrait of the bishop on another wall. A crucifix hung on the wall above the buffet. The sun was shining through the windows and brightened up the room, which would have been dreary with the dark paneling and furniture. There were crystal lamps and vases and dishes placed here and there, all of good quality, some quite old. A small, aging photograph of an elderly man and woman rested on the buffet. The resemblance of the old man to the priest was striking. It was obviously his father.

"I hope you didn't mind my teasing you at dinner the other night," Joshua said to the priest.

"Not at all. I enjoyed it. It brought out a side of your personality I had not seen before. It was a good evening. Everyone enjoyed themselves. You seemed to be enjoying the evening yourself."

"Yes, I did. It is good to see the clergy having a good time together. Do the other clergy associate?" Joshua asked, concerned.

"No. They're a little stuffy, if I must say so. Russ and I became fast friends as soon as he moved here. The others get together occasionally. They are friendly enough, but are usually a bit distant. I think it's more their people who don't approve of their fraternizing. Things are too tense here, and they are afraid of being drawn into something they can't handle. So they keep their distance. Russ and I are always in the thick of things with our own people so we don't have much choice but to be in the middle of trouble. It's a blessing we are such good friends. It helps us to keep a steady rein on our people, most of them anyway."

"Most of them?" Joshua asked, surprised.

"Yes, there are some who are radical. They've been a

thorn in my side all my life. They're not religious, but use religion as their front. Most of them haven't darkened the doors of the church since they were kids. That priest I told you about, they meet with him regularly when he passes through town. I guess he's the spark behind a lot of their doings. They get their arms from that Muslim family that lives in the neighborhood. I guess you know them. You helped their boy who was blinded when they were unloading a shipment of arms on the coast a while back."

"Yes," Joshua commented. "I was at their house the other night. They are nice people, and I think perhaps they may be changed in their way of looking at things."

"You may be right. The father came in to talk to me yesterday and asked if he could borrow a Bible. He had read the Gospels a long time ago and would like to read them again but didn't have a copy at home. I let him take mine. He said you reminded him a lot of Jesus."

Joshua blushed. The priest looked at him, curious, thinking hard about what the Muslim had said. He had wondered himself about Joshua, but didn't dare to entertain the thought. It seemed too preposterous. The thought, however, crossed his mind more and more.

Marie brought in the breakfast. The priest invited her to sit down and have breakfast with them. He knew how much she liked Joshua and would be thrilled just to be able to have the memory of having breakfast with him. At first she was reluctant, then she agreed, and sat across from Joshua. She was a bit embarrassed, but Joshua soon put her at ease, asking her questions about herself and her family. Before long she was telling him everything about her life. After a few minutes she excused herself, saying she had work to do.

Joshua and the priest continued their conversation,

the priest wondering about the newspaper article and what it meant in terms of Joshua's strategy. "Joshua, I know you're aware that that newspaper story has already reached a lot of homes and by now has stirred a considerable amount of discussion. Not all of it is going to be favorable. You can expect strange people to be passing through here just to see what's going on and to figure out how they want to deal with you. You realize that, I'm sure. For every fifty people who may approve of what you're doing, there will be a hothead who will be driven to near apoplexy over it. I am so afraid for you and, I must add, also for the children."

"Elmer, don't worry about the children. They will be safe. Nothing will happen to them. Remember what it says in the Gospels, 'Not one of those you have given me will be lost'? Well, it applies here. Not one of the children will be hurt. So lay your fears to rest. I know my Father and he has willed it this way. It is the only way."

"Young man," the priest said, finishing his coffee, "I hope you're right. Still, be careful. I have work to do and I know you have your work cut out for you today, so we better get started."

They both got up from the table and walked through the kitchen to say good-bye to Marie. Joshua then left. Elmer watched him with a look of sadness in his eyes as he walked out through the rose garden. He was clearly concerned about the future and about this strange young man he had grown so fond of . . . and perhaps not without good reason.

Joshua arrived at the square around the same time as usual. Children were already waiting. Some had clippings from the newspaper they were excited to show him.

"Joshua," Peter called to him as he walked slowly

across the square, "did you see the paper, and the article about you in it, and about me and Acmet?"

"I didn't read it all. What does it say? Tell me about it."

"No, Joshua, you have to read it. It's a good article," Peter insisted.

Joshua took the clipping from Peter and began reading it. The article started by describing Joshua, his appearance, his manners, and the effect he had on the crowd of children who followed him, then went on to say:

It is not difficult to see what this man Joshua is attempting to do, clearly the impossible. His strategy is faultless. The loyalty of the children, who literally follow him everywhere and hang on to his every word, is absolute. If what this man is trying to accomplish takes hold, it is capable of transforming the whole country. The march on the city a few days ago has already sparked children's interest in other places, and small groups of Catholic and Protestant children are associating with each other for the first time in their lives. The reaction of parents is mixed. Some think it is beautiful, some are troubled over it, radicals are clearly disturbed, realizing the movement's potential for undermining their cause, which can succeed only if they can pass on their hatred to the next generation. Whether this simple idealist's dream will be allowed to continue is the big question. Only time will answer that.

Then there was the little story about Peter and his blind friend, Acmet. The reporter did a good job of interviewing the two children.

When Joshua finished speaking to the children, they walked away. Two youngsters stayed. One was holding the other by the hand. I could see one boy was blind. The blind boy's name was Acmet. His friend's name was Peter. In talking to the boys I found that the blind boy was an Arab whose family was living in the village. Peter was waiting for Joshua to finish so he could ask him if he could cure his friend's blindness. Whether he ever did I was unable to find out. What was touching was the complete trust these children had in this man who was but a total stranger only a few weeks before. One boy was a Catholic, the other was a Muslim. The boy wasn't asking for anything for himself but for a favor for his Muslim friend. One could readily see how this simple stranger was capable of setting the world upside down.

Joshua gave the clipping back to Peter with the comment "The man did a good job writing the article. It should go far in helping to spread the good news. The article about you and Acmet was very well done. You should be proud of yourselves. Now you can see how unselfish love of others can touch people's hearts and inspire them to goodness."

The children were happy this morning. They were more interested in the picture the reporter had taken of the group standing around listening to Joshua, and trying to identify themselves in the photograph, than they were in the article.

Joe came up to Joshua with his trumpet tucked under his arm and looking very concerned. He asked Joshua what the reporter meant when he asked whether people would allow them to continue. Joshua tried to explain. "Don't you worry about that, Joe. That's God's business. We will do just what God wants, and he will see to it that the good he intends will be accomplished. It will go on until all that God intends is completed. No one can stop what we are doing. God will not be frustrated by mean people's schemes. That is definite. So there is no need ever to worry when you are doing good. God will see to its success. You must always trust God and have patience."

Joshua could explain the most profound workings of God's mind in ways that even these little children could understand. He had that knack of making sense out of religion so kids could find meaning and pleasure in it.

Joe had a little surprise for Joshua and for the group. His friend he had been teaching to play the trumpet was going to play for Joshua. The boy was a little embarrassed at first, then, after he started playing, forgot himself and played beautifully a piece from Haydn that Joe had been secretly teaching him. The boy made only one little mistake, which wasn't very noticeable. Everyone was impressed and clapped loudly when he finished.

Then it was Joshua's turn. He took the trumpet, put it to his mouth, and smiled, knowing full well he wasn't going to do nearly as well as the little boy. He started to play and played a simple melody Joe had been trying to teach him. He sounded better but still needed a lot more practice, Joe told him. Joshua agreed. He promised to try harder, especially when he saw that the kids really wanted him to play well. He hadn't taken his playing too seriously.

The children stayed with Joshua until noontime, then went home. Joshua went off into the meadow and wandered through the fields, thinking, relaxing, and contemplating nature, absorbing the presence of his Father in the beautiful world surrounding him. Sometimes Joe would bring him lunch, sometimes he forgot. This day he forgot. Joshua was unconcerned. At two o'clock he left the meadow and walked up to the blacksmith's shop. Charlie was glad to see him, relieved that he could take a break.

"That was quite an article about you in the newspaper. You're a real celebrity now." Joshua thanked him and just shrugged.

"All part of the day's work," Joshua said as he put on his apron. Charlie gave him a list of the things he needed and asked if he minded if he went home for a while. Joshua didn't mind at all. He would have everything done when he returned. Joshua dived right into the work, hammering each piece into perfect shape and laying it aside, then going on to the next piece. He worked with a rare precision, using the tools with such an ease and care that when each piece was finished it looked like it had come out of a machine. By the time Charlie returned Joshua had made a whole order of door hinges, rims for wagon wheels, a number of horseshoes all ready for shoeing, and a fancy doorstop with a fine personal touch to it that fascinated Charlie.

Charlie couldn't believe Joshua was able to do all that he had done while he was away. "With help like that, I'll be caught up in a couple of weeks. I can't thank you enough, young man. Do you want your pay now or at the end of the week?"

"The end of the week is all right. I don't need it right now."

When Joshua left he was tired. He walked out across the field to the pond to take a swim and wash his clothes. The afternoon was hot, which made the water all the more refreshing. Afterward he fell sound asleep on the grass and didn't wake up until a flock of sheep came over to graze all around him. He sat up quietly so as not to frighten them, and when they came close he petted them, holding them affectionately by the ears. Then he got up and walked across to Tim's house to take him up on his invitation to dinner. Tim was thrilled, and so were the others. They, too, had read the article in the newspaper and couldn't wait to talk to him about it.

Joshua stayed there for the night. It was a happy ending to a fruitful day.

EACH succeeding day became more complicated for Joshua, even as his work with the children became more enjoyable. The children and Joshua had grown close during the short time he had been in town, but as interest in what he was doing spread, people's involvement became more personal. Strangers came drifting into town from all over the country to get a glimpse of this unusual man and what he was all about. Some wanted to talk to him and spend time with him personally. Others were content to just watch and analyze. Some looked friendly. Others were clearly hostile. Two clergymen particularly, who had close ties to groups in the town, came to visit at different times, each with a band of local followers. One of the clergymen was a priest, a Roman Catholic; the other was a Presbyterian minister. The priest, Father Jack Brown, was the one Father Donnelly had warned Joshua about, whose clandestine activities were a cause of deep concern to the old priest. The other clergyman was the one Joshua had heard speak at the park a few weeks earlier. He was the kind of person everyone feared. Both men were fanatics, both filled with deep hatred and suspicions that they succeeded well in communicating to their followers.

On the occasion of Father Brown's visit, Joshua was

talking to the children in the square. The priest and his handful of shabbily dressed cronies stood at a distance, just far enough away to hear all of Joshua's conversations with the children. The men's rage at seeing the Catholic and Protestant children having such a good time together was obvious. They never approached Joshua, never introduced themselves to him, just listened and took notes, then walked away, talking excitedly among themselves. As they walked out of the square the priest was silent. His sullen, tense features reflected the dark, ominous thoughts that were festering within.

The visit of the Presbyterian minister was similar. He came with his band of cronies, stood off at a distance, watching, listening, calculating, and wandering off like the others, deep in dark thoughts. Joshua noticed both groups when they came. A sadness crossed his calm features. While seemingly absorbed in talking to the children, his memories roamed across the centuries, recalling pharisees and scribes in flowing robes sprinkled throughout crowds of his followers, listening, watching, calculating in just the same manner and with the same dark countenances worn by these men. It bode ill for the future. He realized there will always be those so stuck in their own narrow, myopic interests, whether it be theology or politics, that they feel threatened by people growing in love and understanding of one another. It is too threatening to their own narrow schemes, which can thrive only where there are clearly defined and impenetrable political or theological barriers. Their sick, disturbed personalities thrive on conflict, which can't cope with acceptance and understanding. While seemingly struggling for peace, they could never function once there is peace, and they become unglued at the prospect of imminent peace becoming a reality.

And now, as in the past, the serenity of Joshua's manner was unruffled in the face of churning tempests. His confidence in his Father's plans gave him all the assurance he needed to remain resolute in his purpose. The prospect of impending danger or even tragedy never became an overwhelming obsession. His trust in his Father's closeness was absolute, so all that the children saw amid the flurry of new activity in town was the same peaceful, tranquil, carefree man they loved. Everything went on as before. The children reflected in their behavior Joshua's own security.

In the afternoons Joshua went to the blacksmith's place, still helping him catch up on his work. Charlie was appreciative and offered to pay Joshua well, but Joshua declined to accept all he offered, saying he really didn't need that much. The old man was surprised, not offended, and looked upon Joshua's declining the money as a show of friendship, so he invited him to his house for supper, which Joshua readily accepted.

When Charlie saw how clever Joshua was at shaping the iron, he asked him to make some special pieces for himself, his wife, and his friends. Joshua was delighted to oblige him and spent three whole afternoons crafting imaginative articles that became a source of pride to the old craftsman.

Days passed. Mornings with the children were much the same. Strangers passed through the village, curious after reading the news article, eager to see with their own eyes if Joshua's project really worked. That was one thing no one could deny. It really did work, perhaps too well for

Joshua's own good. Afternoons at the blacksmith shop were fun. Joshua had his own techniques and tricks for drawing, twisting, hammering, and shearing the hot iron into intricate and unusual shapes, giving the finished products an almost delicate quality.

One afternoon the Reverend Davis came down to watch Joshua. Charlie was one of his parishioners and he, too, had told his pastor about Joshua.

"You sure are a talented man, Joshua," Russ commented as he watched Joshua shaping the white-hot metal.

"This is fun," Joshua retorted. "It's the kind of thing everyone would enjoy doing. It's perfect for keeping in shape."

"Where did you learn how to do this kind of work?" Russ asked.

"Oh, I learned it a long time ago, growing up. I always enjoyed it but didn't do it for very long," Joshua responded without going into detail.

The minister picked up a finished piece that had already cooled, turned it over in his hand, looked at it from different angles, and remarked over the fineness of the workmanship.

"Thank you," Joshua said humbly. "Can I make something for you? I'm sure Charlie wouldn't mind."

"I'd like that," the minister answered.

"No, I wouldn't mind at all," Charlie said. "I enjoy watching him myself, and I've been doing it all my life."

While the two men watched Joshua took a piece of hot iron, put it on a flat surface, and started hammering it into shape, then reheating it, hammering it again, and carefully poking pieces out, forming an intricate pattern in the metal, then carefully shaping the delicate sections with the calipers and a stylus-like rod. In no time he had formed a beautifully designed trivet for Russ to give to his wife for use in the kitchen. When it cooled Charlie painted it for him. Joshua then proceeded to make a pair of bookends for the minister. Into the left bookend Joshua carefully carved with calipers a replica of the tablets of the Ten Commandments with a crack in them. Into the right bookend he carved the same tablets but in such a way as to take the form of a heart, symbolizing the New Law in Christ's love. The bookends looked almost molded they were so perfect. They were heavy, but with a finished and exquisite look about them.

"There, my good friend," Joshua said as he placed the cooled and painted pieces on the counter, "the old ways must go, the new way must take hold in people's hearts."

Russ was thrilled. Charlie was too. And so was Joshua. He was always happiest doing nice things for people.

Russ left, a little embarrassed nobody would take any money from him, but as he walked down the street he was like a child who has just been given a Christmas present.

When they closed the shop Charlie insisted Joshua come home with him for dinner so they could bring the special pieces home together. The house wasn't far from the shop, so they were there in no time, carrying big, heavy boxes full of things Joshua had made.

Charlie's wife, Margaret, had just come back from shopping and met them at the kitchen door.

"What do you fellows have there?" she said for conversation.

"A surprise," Charlie said as they all walked into the house together.

"I can't wait to see them," she responded.

Inside, she turned on the lights and made room for the boxes on the kitchen table. The men put them down and took a deep breath. The boxes were heavy.

One by one Charlie took the presents out of the boxes, giving Margaret hers.

"They're beautiful," she raved, thrilled with the delicacy of the pieces. "I have never seen work so fine, and Charlie's the best. He's always so busy making things for customers, he doesn't get a chance to make nice things like this."

"I couldn't do it even if I tried," Charlie admitted humbly. "Joshua's a master."

Joshua said nothing, just smiled, happy he had made the couple so happy.

The two men washed up and went out on the porch to rest while Margaret prepared supper. In no time Charlie was asleep, snoring. Joshua rocked back and forth in his rocking chair, taking in the scenery, resting his tired muscles. It was a warm evening, but a cool breeze drifted across the fields and through the yard. The sun was settling down over the distant hills, casting long shadows across the fields. Birds were flying frantically, catching insects in flight. There was a soft, golden glow in the atmosphere. It was quiet and peaceful.

Charlie woke up when Margaret called for supper. A little embarrassed, he apologized for going to sleep on his guest. Joshua laughed, not the slightest bit offended. The two men went into the house for supper. Margaret had the table set impeccably, wanting to make a good impression on their guest and also show her appreciation for all that he was doing to help her husband.

It was a simply prepared meal, potatoes and steak, which she had bought in the hope Charlie would be bringing Joshua home for dinner. The conversation at the table was simple. They were not intellectual people and their interests were limited to things happening around the village and how business had changed over the years. Fortunately the couple had put money aside when they realized the blacksmith business no longer had the demand it used to, and they could rest comfortably as business slowed.

After supper they all helped with the dishes, against Margaret's strong objections, then went out and sat on the porch talking and sipping tea until a little after sunset. At Charlie's insistence, Joshua stayed for the night.

CHAPTER 25

THE EFFECTS of the newspaper article were beginning to show. To the children in various places around the country Joshua was fast becoming their hero, although most had never seen him, had no idea what he looked like, or even who he really was. In places far from the village Catholic and Protestant children decided to ignore the ancient taboo of forced isolation from one another. A few groups of private school officials decided to open their schools to children of all religions. The response was immediate. Many people, just itching for the chance, began signing up their children. It took courage, but so many were so fed up with the incessant fighting and hatred, they were willing to try anything to bring peace back into their lives and prepare a better future for their children.

Follow-up news articles showed graphically how the movement was spreading, in little pockets at first, then to larger villages and towns, and even to the cities. No terrorist would dare violate children. It would show only too pointedly who the enemy really was and permanently seal their doom. Children even began going with their new friends to each others' churches, something unheard of. The clergy, even well-intentioned ones, became nervous over that but did not dare to say a word publicly. Politicians

were either tongue-tied or speechless when interviewed by
the press, not knowing how to react. They were trapped.
To approve of what was happening would enrage their
constituents, whose puppets they were. To criticize the
children's innocent show of concern would strip naked
their bad faith and secret meanness. They said nothing,
but seethed inside.

Joshua's friends showed him the articles. He read them
carefully, with a broad smile lighting up his face. "God
bless the children. Now if they would only start the same
war against drugs," Joshua mused, half to himself. "The
children have the potential to bring sanity and restore
goodness to a sick world."

People from widely scattered places began coming to
talk with Joshua, a new kind of people, different from
others who had been coming. These were good people with
social standing and with resources. Some offered their
help, some offered money. Some asked what he thought
they could do in their own way back home. To each
Joshua's answer was the same: "Work for peace by rising
above the pettiness of life and never taking offense. Be
kind to those who are miserable. Show appreciation to
those who do good work. Respect the dignity of each
person. Heal wounds wherever you find hurt. Do whatever
you can to comfort those who are troubled. Replace anger
and suspicion with understanding. It doesn't take money.
It takes love and concern."

Joshua's message was simple, just like himself, much
like the message taught so very long ago, a message that
was never taken seriously and yet had the potential to heal
the world's ills.

One day two bishops came to town. Surprisingly, they
came together, one Roman Catholic, the other Anglican.

They had contacted their respective clergy in the village a day before to announce their coming. They would like very much to visit with this man Joshua if that could be arranged. They would also like, out of courtesy, to visit with the other clergy in the village, since they all had serious interests in common. Both churches made hurried preparations to host both men jointly and provide for their accommodations.

Father Donnelly took a rare walk down to the square to invite Joshua up to the house to meet the bishops. The Anglican priest invited the Wesleyan minister, John Cooke, and his wife, as well as Russ and his wife and Elmer, to the parish house for the dinner that evening.

Bishop Edmund Chalmers, the Anglican bishop, was a chubby, friendly man, with features that betrayed a life filled with troubles. The man had a broad respect from all decent-thinking people and a reputation for fairness. Bishop Charles Ryan, the Roman Catholic, was a tough-looking man who could have passed for a boxer, but a man who had a reputation for high intelligence and good humor, a man whose one ambition was to heal the terrible rift that plagued the country. The radicals of his own religion had little use for him. To them he was as dangerous as the enemy. The bishop said what he had to say and was totally unafraid of any possible recriminations.

Joshua's first contact with the two bishops occurred while he was talking with the children in the square. The bishops had stopped off first at Father Donnelly's place, left their car there, and walked down to the square, hoping to observe Joshua in action.

When they entered the square the children were just finishing their informal music session. Joshua was still trying to play the trumpet. The children were laughing good-naturedly at the mistakes he was making. It was all part of Joshua's lesson. When he finished he gave the instrument back to Joe, promising that one day he would give them a surprise. One of the older boys who had come recently played the guitar, making up songs for everyone to sing. One was about Joshua and his message of peace. Joshua sat down on the wall and listened as the children sang and the boy strummed his guitar.

When they finished he told them to be seated. Still sitting on the wall, he said to them, "See what beautiful harmony your lives are creating. That music is just an outward expression of the real harmony that is forming in your hearts.

"God formed you with tender love, and just like he loves and cares for you, so he wants you to have the same love and care for one another. When you choose to approach God alone he will say to you, 'Where are your brothers and sisters?' And if you have walked away from them and have not made them part of your life, then you go to God with your work unfinished. Your work on earth is to help form and perfect the family of God and, by sharing the gifts God gave you, fill up in the lives of others those things they lack. In that you will find your happiness on earth and earn your reward with God in heaven."

The two bishops were impressed with what Joshua said, and having picked up a sense of what his intentions were, they walked from the square back down to the priest's house.

Father Donnelly was picking roses to decorate the house when the two men arrived. Getting up from his knees with difficulty, he welcomed them and escorted them into the house.

"I am honored that you came to visit us. I hope you

enjoy your little visit. Come right in. I assume your curiosity got the best of you and you took a walk to the square to see Joshua."

"Yes, we did," Bishop Chalmers answered. "And I must admit, I was quite impressed."

"As was I," Bishop Ryan added. "That man is quite an individual. I had the strangest feeling I was living in the midst of a real-life gospel story."

"That's strange," Elmer added, "because when he comes to the church to visit some mornings, I have the exact same feeling. The way he speaks, his tone of voice, his profound sense of peace, everything about him suggests that it couldn't be much different if Christ himself were right here. And I don't even feel guilty thinking that way."

In the house, Marie had anticipated their coming and had a snack already prepared for them. Elmer ushered them into the living room and seated them while Marie prepared to serve the refreshments.

The bishops did not take long to get around to the point of their visit. They wanted to experience Joshua firsthand and ask the local clergy for their sense of what Joshua was doing. Was it reasonable? Did it make sense? Or was it just a passing phenomenon that had no possibility of taking any real root?

Elmer answered those concerns emphatically. "No, I don't think this is just a flash in a pan. There's a depth and a sense of purpose to that young man that gives even cynics the feeling he knows he's going to succeed in what he has set out to accomplish. And he is brutally realistic. He knows full well that there are some who will be determined not to let his project continue, yet he knows in some way that nothing is going to prevent him from accomplishing what he has set out to do."

"And what is that?" Bishop Ryan asked pointedly.

"It is obvious. He has a long-range plan to short-circuit the violence that has become a disease in these parts. The route he has chosen is through the children. If he can get them to mingle and become friends, and can get this to spread, he knows it will succeed. I have to admit he's shrewd in the way he's going about it. He never does a thing to antagonize anyone. He's quiet, gentle, friendly, and, in the short time he's been here, knows half the town. He even cured a Muslim boy of blindness last week. The kid's father came in later and asked for a copy of the Gospels. I think we can feel quite safe with this fellow. I encourage my people to back him, and so does Russ Davis, the Presbyterian pastor. He thinks he's the greatest thing that's hit the country."

"What about the Anglican priest?" Bishop Chalmers asked.

"He hasn't said anything against him, but I really don't know how he feels personally about what he's doing. He's in a little different situation than Russ and myself. Our people are in the midst of things. His people are a bit more isolated."

"On the way down here Bishop Ryan and I were talking about making a public statement supporting what this man Joshua is doing in the hope that it can spread to the rest of the country. It might just work. If all the churches can work together on it, then it can happen that much faster. We want to get a feeling from yourself and the other pastors as to how you would feel about our support."

"I really can't speak for the others, but I think your support would be magnificent. It certainly can't do any harm, and it will reassure parents who might be concerned about letting their children become involved."

At that point the doorbell rang. Marie answered it and brought Joshua into the room. Everyone automatically stood up, not knowing why. Elmer introduced Joshua to the two bishops, and they all sat down.

"Our celebrity!" Bishop Ryan exclaimed. Joshua blushed.

"We were just talking about you, young man," the bishop continued. "Bishop Chalmers and I were impressed with the way you handled that rather large group of kids. Not too many could exercise that kind of control over children."

"I've always loved children," Joshua responded. "They are innocent and unspoiled, as they came from the hand of God. It is grown-ups who steer them in wrong directions."

"Joshua," Bishop Chalmers interjected, "why do you think your work with the children will succeed?"

"That's simple. It is the will of my Father, and his will will not be frustrated. He loves these people, and although they have been made to fear one another, they are all victims. They didn't create this situation. They inherited it and don't know any way out of it. The way I have chosen is the only way. It will succeed."

"Can we help?" Bishop Ryan asked.

"Yes, by encouraging others not to be afraid but to allow their children to reach out to others like they have here. In time they will learn to trust and become friends. They are the adults of the future. If they learn trust now, they will carry it with them through life."

It was all so simple. The bishops were glad they had

come. They were glad Joshua had stopped by. They were grateful for the courageous work he was attempting to do and assured him of their supoprt. Joshua excused himself and left.

The bishops had accomplished what they had come for and were anxious to visit the Anglican rector and meet over dinner with the others later in the evening. They got up to leave, thanking Marie for her hospitality, and walked to the door with the pastor. Elmer accompanied them to the car and said he was looking forward to dinner that evening.

J. Stanford Crist, or J.C., as his friends called him, had been rector at All Saints for over twelve years. He was tall, thin, scholarly-looking, and affable. His wife, Norma, not quite as tall, was round-faced and jolly. They were a happy couple and had survived in the village by keeping pretty much to themselves and becoming involved only in the lives of their parishioners, who had grown accustomed to their discreet, personable ways. Father Crist had taught in the seminary for over fifteen years before taking this assignment in the village. It was a pleasant assignment for a rector who could enjoy being a diplomat and had the discipline not to be drawn into the local politics.

If the rector was not overly warm in his relationships with the other clergy, it was not out of snobbishness but for the sake of his survival. It was his long-standing policy not to become involved in any relationships that would embroil him in the highly complicated tensions of the community, which could explode at any time and without warning. This uninvolvement was the reason he was still there after twelve years. His predecessors had not been as discreet or as fortunate. They had lasted only a few years.

The joint visit of the two bishops made Father Crist

uncomfortable. He knew both of them by reputation, and his own bishop by close association on the seminary faculty, where he had been nicknamed "The Roman Rector of Canterbury." The two bishops were great friends and conferred on every decision each of them made. He strongly suspected why the two of them had come here together and did not like it one bit.

When the two bishops arrived in early afternoon, Father Crist met them at the door and welcomed them graciously. They congratulated him on the meticulous care he had obviously taken of the gardens and the buildings. Every rector should be as attentive to the surroundings of God's home. The comments were appreciated, and the rector conducted the two men into the parish house and introduced them to his wife, who was busy preparing a light midday luncheon for everyone.

After the formalities the priest showed the two men to their rooms upstairs, offering them the option of either staying upstairs to relax and freshen up before lunch or, if they preferred, coming down to the study to socialize. They said they would be down presently.

In the few minutes before lunch the socializing was more like shadowboxing. Bishop Chalmers asked Father Crist how he felt about Joshua. The rector had no strong feelings one way or another.

"Surely you've heard of him?" the bishop remarked rather caustically, revealing a long-standing tension between the two men.

"Of course I've heard of him, but I've made a point of not involving myself in politics around here."

"But from what I've gathered, this man Joshua is far from political. He seems to be a thoroughly dedicated Christian trying rather heroically, if I must say, to do a job that should have been done by the clergy long before this."

"You may look at it that way, Bishop, but I live here and I see things much differently. I see Joshua as a man who is totally political, maybe for religious motives and with good intentions, but political nonetheless."

Bishop Ryan felt it would have been better if he had stayed upstairs, feeling this was a private matter between the two Anglicans. Bishop Chalmers, realizing he had not put his best foot forward, tried to lighten the conversation without changing the subject, which he intended to pursue.

"J.C.," he said, adopting a more familiar tone, "I can see how he can be construed as political. His goal is certainly not going to endear him to radicals on either side, but how do you think the ordinary people view him?"

"Well, that may be a different question. My own people seem to like him. In fact, knowing that Father Donnelly and the Presbyterian minister have had him to dinner, my people have been pressuring me to do the same. I would like to meet him. He seems like a rather interesting chap."

"That might be a good thing, having him for dinner sometime. He does seem to deserve our united support," the bishop added casually. At that point they broke for lunch.

Norma's presence at lunch had a tempering effect on the conversation. The clerics did not feel as free to pursue the matter in front of the rector's wife. The occasion turned into a delightful social hour, which put everyone in a much better frame of mind to discuss more freely later on what the two visitors had on their minds.

In the afternoon the bishops retired to their rooms and rested, leaving the rector free to finish the work he had originally scheduled for the day. He was glad when they went upstairs.

26

BY SEVEN O'CLOCK people were arriving at the parish house for dinner. Russ and his wife were unable to come. They were out of town for the day. Elmer, always promptly on time, was the first one to arrive. The two senior wardens and their wives came a few minutes later. They were all escorted into the study, which was cozier and more relaxing than the parlor. Father Crist was an excellent host and had everyone's drink already prepared, knowing from past parties each one's preference, except for Bishop Ryan, who said he would like a martini. Norma had made a huge tray of hors d'oeuvres, which she brought out and placed on a serving table strategically positioned for everyone's convenience.

Cocktail time was light and jovial. No one talked about anything heavy. Everyone just coasted into a warm, friendly mood that lasted for a good part of the evening and opened the way for a relaxed setting in which to discuss business later on.

The wardens and their wives had never met the Roman Catholic bishop before, though they had heard much about him in the news and had read some of his statements, which they agreed must have taken no small amount of courage to express. The bishop didn't think of himself as being terribly heroic. It was, he felt, just part of his job and something that he should do if he wanted to be able to live with himself. Whatever his motives, they still admired his strong stand on issues. That is the mark of a good leader, one of the wardens said in a not so subtle swipe at the rector's refusal to take a strong stand on issues they deemed important.

It was not lost on Father Crist or the others. Everyone was gracious enough to let it pass without comment. Elmer remarked it would have been nice to have Joshua at the dinner.

"That fellow sure does know how to handle himself, even socially," Elmer interjected. "You would think a person as single-minded as he is would be a bit gauche at social affairs, but not that one. He's as quick as a flash and has a playful sense of humor. You should see the tricks he can do with just an ordinary rubber ball. I don't know whether it's an illusion or something else, but he had us all acting like kids with what he did with the thing."

"Do you feel comfortable with what he's doing, Elmer?" Bishop Ryan asked.

"Yes, I do," the priest answered. "I feel comfortable with him because he's so methodical and circumspect. He makes you feel comfortable by communicating an uncanny sense that what he is doing is what God wants him to do. And he's not a disturbed person. He's very sane and very realistic. He talks about his work as being his father's will. It gives you a strange feeling when he talks like that, because you can't help but see the striking similarity between the way he talks and the way Jesus used to talk. Sometimes I even wonder . . . but then at times I feel it's not right to think that way."

The guests were so engrossed in their lively discussion about Joshua that no one paid much attention to the meal, though everyone was enjoying what they were eating and absentmindedly taking second helpings.

Norma would have felt slighted over her guests paying such little attention to what she had spent so long preparing for them except that they were all eating nonstop, which was the best show of approval because it was not contrived.

"The reason we are here," Bishop Chalmers remarked, "is to discuss what Joshua is doing. What that man has accomplished is having widespread consequences all across the country. There's something more than a mere natural phenomenon we are experiencing. If it is the work of God, as Joshua seems so convinced, then it behooves all of us, as religious and community leaders, to lend our support and make sure it takes hold. It may be the only chance we have to end this senseless scandal of Christians killing one another."

Everyone was quiet, looking furtively at one another, afraid to be the first to comment on the bishop's remark. To show support for his colleague, Bishop Ryan added his concerns: "Yes, this is something we all have to search our souls over. It is not right to let this total stranger stick his neck out to do something that should be the responsibility of us all. It shames us as Christian leaders to just stand by, secure in our own comfortable towers, and watch this brave fellow do what we should be doing, making efforts to resolve this problem, which has become a disgrace to our religion and an insult to Christ."

Elmer nodded approval. The senior wardens were also inclined to agree but were reluctant to embarrass their rector, who was already considerably uneasy over the direction the conversation had taken. He knew it was going to come around to something like this and was afraid of what concrete measures the bishops were going to pop on them.

One of the wardens, uncomfortable with the sudden lull in the conversation, asked the bishop what he had in mind.

That was the opening he needed and one that the rector shrewdly would not give him. "Something simple but practical. The people have to know where we stand. If we speak out in support of what Joshua is doing, then we lend credence to his work. That will have incalculable effects on those who are still on the fence. Bishop Ryan has a reputation for being judicious and outspoken. My own reputation is much the same, so people will listen. On the way down this morning we agreed to write a joint pastoral letter saying that we approve of what Joshua is doing and recommending the wholehearted support of all of our people. When we do this it is imperative that we have the support of our clergy here in the village, because the press will be looking for an immediate response from the local clergy. If you are not one hundred percent behind our statement, it will confuse the people and negate our own efforts. What I am trying to say is that we were hoping you could see your way clear to endorsing our expression of support."

No one knew what to say. Elmer had already given his support. The whole village knew where he stood on the matter, so he felt it was not his place to speak up now. Norma felt sorry for her husband. He was in the frying pan.

"Bishop," the rector finally said very slowly and in measured words, "I have spent my whole life trying to be careful, thinking it is the way expected of me. At times I felt I should be more forthright, but all in all my prudence has kept my people from becoming embroiled in the highly charged tensions in the community. For me to change now would not be in the best interests of my people."

"What do you see as the best interests of your people at a time like this, when the whole country is being torn apart? Security for our people is sometimes an interest we can ill afford when the country itself is being engulfed in a fratricidal war. Security under those conditions is merely an illusion. Everyone will be caught up in the conflagration if it burns out of control, and it will be the fault of those who could have done something and chose to protect themselves. With every killing the hatred multiplies by the number of people in the victim's family plus their friends. In time every family will be affected. It has to stop somewhere. Staying aloof is a luxury we can no longer afford."

The Methodist minister felt the same way J.C. felt. Why look for trouble? They had their flocks to think about. If other people were fighting, why should they become involved? Their strategy of noninvolvement had worked well for all these years, why change now? They admired Joshua for what he was doing, but that was his choice.

"If it works," John Cooke finished by saying, "all well and good, but if it doesn't, he can walk off and leave us all to clean up the streets."

The bishops hadn't come just to hear objections, and they were not going to leave until they had everyone's support.

"Gentlemen, I realize John and his wife are Methodists, and we are grateful he and his wife came this evening, and it is not our intention to preempt your superiors, John, but Bishop Ryan and I wanted to express to all of you in the village, out of courtesy, our intention of making a joint statement encouraging our people to act positively and together in this matter. And we feel it is important for as many as possible to be with us."

Father Crist agreed to consider the matter seriously and certainly would do nothing to show opposition. Elmer gave his wholehearted support. John Cooke expressed appreciation to J.C. for inviting him, and said he would work with him on the matter and that they would do jointly whatever they could agree on. With that expression of at least goodwill, the bishops let the matter drop for the evening and went on to discuss more enjoyable topics.

The evening ended amicably, and by the time everyone retired the bishops felt pretty sure they had at least a more solid support than when they came.

CHAPTER 27

THE BISHOPS left the next
morning with at least a tacit assurance that the rector
would support their proposed statement. Russ had heard
about the dinner the night before and felt more disappointed than ever that he had been unable to attend. He
did call Bishop Chalmers and tell him of his willingness to
give total support to whatever the two bishops might
propose in their joint pastoral letter. The bishops spent the
better part of the next two weeks drawing up the letter.
Their advisers read it, made suggestions for minor changes
here and there, and offered advice as to the timing of its
release. A Friday was chosen for maximum press coverage
and to allow the clergy to prepare comments for the
following Sunday.

The pastoral letter received front-page coverage in the
secular press and rave editorials from most newspapers.
Some were highly critical, however, saying the bishops'
ideas were unrealistic and might in the long haul occasion
more harm than good. A surprising source of support came
from youth groups of various denominations, praising the
two leaders for their rare courage in taking such a strong
position, and encouraging all their members to take the
recommendations of the bishops to heart and reach out to

young people of other denominations and form bonds of friendship and cooperation with those whose friendship had always been forbidden. A follow-up of Joshua's work was included in related articles in various papers.

The very day the statement was issued reporters appeared at rectory doorsteps in the village requesting interviews with the pastors of the different churches. To a man they were all supportive, even J. Stanford Crist, who issued a beautifully worded expression of support for the pastoral letter, praising the bishops "not just for the courage of their stand on this issue, but for the far-reaching implications of their joint statement in the whole area of ecumenical relations. The two men have, indeed, taken a giant step forward in making Christianity credible in a world that was fast losing hope." Everyone who knew the rector was impressed.

From the moment the pastoral was released, repercussions were immediate. It gave a notoriety and a credibility to Joshua's existence and his work with the children. Seeing the very positive results the letter was having aroused radicals on both sides. What they thought was a harebrained idea on the part of the oddball idealist now took on dimensions that threatened all their radical schemes. The main source of arms had been cut off when the Muslim family was converted by Joshua and they had become the most enthusiastic of his followers. Joshua was now seen as the most threatening of all their adversaries. What to do about it was fast becoming an obsession.

The radicals had no legitimate platform or vehicle for public expression to counter the massive and very positive coverage Joshua was receiving in the religious and secular press. To threaten children would turn the whole population against them and discredit them in the eyes of decent people everywhere. All they could do was hold hastily organized meetings to discuss strategy.

In the meantime, in the village, things went on as usual. People went to work, the children gathered with Joshua in the square or out in the meadow, strangers still wandered through town hoping to get a glimpse of this man who was turning the world upside down and, if they were lucky, spend a few minutes talking with him.

Rev. Davis met Joshua in the square one morning and invited him up to the manse for a chat. The pastoral letter had been out only two days. Joshua had not as yet seen it, nor the accompanying articles relating to him. It was of little importance for him to read them. In his uncanny foresight he had already anticipated the effects of the articles and the letter and was quietly planning his strategy to handle the problems he knew would be arising from them. He was aware of the secret meetings of the radicals. He was aware also of the limited number of options they had to counter the good things that were taking place all across the country. He was not concerned.

He went to the manse with the minister more for friendship than for any interest in seeing the articles, which Russ couldn't wait to show him. On the way they met the rector of All Saints. He was in a jolly mood, unusual for him.

"Good morning, Russ," Father Crist said. "I can't remember the weather ever being as nice as this for such a long stretch. I hope it lasts."

"J.C.," Russ responded, "have you ever met Joshua?"

The rector was taken back. Here was the man the whole town was talking about, and even he had offered to support, and, and, for the first time, he realized how ridiculous it was for him not even to have met him.

"Joshua, I'm embarrassed that I haven't made any attempt to get acquainted with you, but I am very happy that we finally got a chance to meet. My name is Stanford Crist. My friends call me J.C." Joshua smiled at the coincidence and shook the priest's hand.

"The bishops must think a lot of you to have issued their joint pastoral letter encouraging everyone's support of what you are doing. I know, I for one was a bit surprised at first over what I thought was their haste, but I have come to see that perhaps they may have a point. I finally decided to lend my own support, limited as it may be."

"In promoting worthwhile causes the contribution of each one is important," Joshua replied. "In these troubled times it is essential that everyone play his part. It lends solidarity to the undertaking and shows to radicals there is nowhere they can turn for support or even sympathy. God does not bless violence, nor is the maiming of innocent people condoned by God. Those who commit these evils will have to answer one day for their wanton treatment of God's children. They have completely ignored the Lord's counsels concerning injustice and have committed crimes that cry to God for vengeance."

The two men were taken back by the sharpness of Joshua's words. The rector blushed, thinking that Joshua was aware of his attitude of noninvolvement.

The men chatted briefly for a few more minutes about lighter topics. Father Crist invited Joshua to his house for dinner at his convenience. The men then parted, Joshua and Russ continuing on their way to the manse.

It was quiet at the manse. Russ's wife was not at home. The two men pored over the newspapers, noting the reactions of various editors to the pastoral letter and the tone of the news articles about Joshua's work with the children.

"Hey, Joshua, look at this little article!" Russ said excitedly as he showed the piece to his friend.

Joshua read it carefully. "Confidential Sources Reveal Radicals Consider Moves to Counter Children's Campaign." The article, hidden among advertisements on a back page, went on to spell out details of secret meetings that radicals on both sides were having in various parts of the country to offset the effects of the children's involvement in that very serious political issue.

This latest turn of events has put a crimp in the whole thrust of the issue and has taken the momentum away from the terrorists and placed the focus of activity clearly with the children. The scheme is considered by the radicals to be insidious and the greatest threat yet to their cause. Though they are stymied as to how to respond, they know that a response is imperative and at their meetings will be discussing the options.

Joshua said nothing.

"Well, what do you think, Joshua?" Russ asked, curious as to Joshua's reaction.

"It is natural for them to feel the way they do. They have to do something, because this makes them look ridiculous, and fanatics can't stand ridicule. There is, however, nothing they can do to stop this movement. It is God's will." Russ was impressed with Joshua's calmness and assurance.

After combing the papers for other items, Russ brewed a pot of tea and served it with some light pastry while they continued their conversation. Joshua did not stay long. He had to be down at the square to meet with the children.

The two men finished their refreshments and Joshua left.

The children were waiting, more excited than ever on this day. Any of the parents who had reservations about Joshua changed their attitudes after reading the bishops' pastoral letter or hearing their pastors talk about it in church that Sunday. Many of the children were holding clippings from the papers for Joshua to read. When he came into the square the children, holding out their clippings, rushed to him and almost knocked him over. He took one of them, read it fast, and commented on it to the children. Since the children wanted him to have them, he took them and put them all together on the stone wall. He told them he would read them later in the day.

Practically all the children in the village were with Joshua now, even Acmet, who talked about Joshua to everyone. He was mesmerized by him, reporting to his family every detail of what Joshua said and did when he met with the children each day. Occasionally his family would come to the square and listen to Joshua speak. When they went home Anwar would get out his New Testament and read the Gospels carefully, comparing the things Joshua said with the things Jesus had said in the Gospels. He noted the striking similarity, not just in the words, but in the mannerisms and mentality of both. Even the name, Joshua, to a Semite, was striking in its coincidence.

The children, even the little ones, were now caught up in the importance of what Joshua was trying to accomplish in their lives. From listening to their parents speaking at home, and from sermons in the churches this past Sunday, they could sense that they were key players in a real-life drama, a drama that was affecting the whole country. They now not only loved Joshua deeply but felt a new pride in being part of his important work.

The entertainment part of the gatherings was becoming more polished. Knowing that they would be performing for the group each day, the musicians practiced for hours so they could really do a good job. It showed in the quality of their playing. Joe's friend showed marked progress. The guitar players had invited others to learn from them and they formed little ensembles, so they could play together and sound more professional. In each group there was a mixture of Catholic and Protestant children. Joshua still did his trumpet act each day, and each day showed only slight improvement. The children were beginning to think he played poorly intentionally so as not to upstage the children who worked so hard to play well. Joshua promised he would surprise them someday. That day, however, was not forthcoming.

Joshua had noticed a nice turn of events lately. When the group used to break up Catholic children would usually pair off with other Catholic children, and Protestant children would do the same. Now, when Joshua finished with the children, small groups of Catholic and Protestant children would go off together. It wasn't contrived, but spontaneous, showing that the friendships developing were beginning to take hold and show signs of becoming more permanent. Joshua smiled in happy satisfaction.

On this particular day Tim McGirr's little boy, Christopher, came with Peter and Acmet. He was all eyes, overcome with all the activity the other children had become accustomed to. He was enjoying the event and did not have to be very involved in order to be content. He wormed his way up to the front of the group so he could be near Joshua. Joshua spotted him and went out of his way to pay attention to him. Chris felt proud that he would single him out in that big crowd.

At the end of the session Peter and Acmet and Chris stayed to talk to Joshua. Joshua sat against the wall and listened. Peter was the one who always did the talking. Their three families were all having a party together and would like Joshua to come. The McGirrs had become friends with the Muslims only recently, when they heard about Acmet and how the family had grown so close to Joshua. Joshua asked him when they were having the party. It would be on the next Saturday night. He told them he would like very much to go. The three children ran off, delighted, as Joshua started out across the meadow toward the sea.

CHAPTER 28

THERE WERE times when the unseen activity surrounding Joshua was so intense that he felt a need to be alone, to digest all that was taking place, to prepare himself for what he knew was unfolding. Never had anyone so quiet and unassuming affected the lives of so many so deeply, by his mere presence, as did Joshua. It was almost as if he affected change in people's lives just by willing it, because on the surface of his simple life, it would be unimaginable that such ordinary things like talking to little children could have such profound and far-reaching repercussions. Perhaps that is the way it is with pure goodness. It is so rare that when it appears it reaches to the depths of good people's hearts and brings to life the goodness they have been unable to express. It also unleashes forces of evil that will always be threatened by the presence of goodness and feel an inexorable need to destroy it. It was the hidden conflict of these forces that Joshua sensed and had to deal with, thus his need to be alone.

The sea was rough when Joshua arrived at the coast. He walked along the rocks. The wind blew the salty spray against him. His long hair blew carelessly in the wind. His tall, slim, strong physique cut fine lines against the warm blue sky. He walked against the wind. It felt good after the trek across the hot meadow.

After a while the wind died down. Joshua walked out along the cliff close to the sea. Two large rectangular rocks, one lying partially on top of the other, formed a perfect seat. Joshua sat down, rested his elbow on his knee, and sucked a straw he had picked in the fields. The sea was growing calm. White-capped waves moved in measured cadence across the surface of the sea until they mysteriously disappeared as they neared the shore. Joshua watched. His thoughts wandered far away, his eyes looking out into the sea but seeing things far beyond in another world, the world from which he drew his strength, his Father's world. His prayer was quiet, deep, wordless. His gentle, peaceful features gave no hint of the hidden world that coursed through his mind.

Joshua stayed in that position for almost an hour, then stretched, yawned, and stood up. Two men fishing in a small boat waved up to him. They were coming to shore. As they landed on a sandy beach not far from where Joshua was walking, they called him and invited him to eat with them. It was late in the afternoon. The men had had a good day and were delighted to share their catch. Joshua picked some debris from around the shore, enough to make a good fire to roast the fish. With the fire going, the men sat down in the sand and introduced themselves.

"I'm George Cinney," one man said. "I came along for the ride because my friend always gets lost." George was a stocky, muscular man of about fifty-five, with taut features, weather-beaten from many years on the windblown sea. He was quiet but had a salty sense of humor.

"And I'm Ervin Farmer, 'Boots' for short." Boots was

of medium height, sturdily built, with a round, ruddy face and wearing horn-rimmed glasses. He had a wary look in his eyes that easily broke into a winsome smile once he relaxed.

"My name's Joshua," Joshua said simply. They all shook hands.

"What are you doing out this way?" George asked Joshua.

"Just taking a walk to get some time to think," Joshua replied.

"Where are you from?" Ervin asked.

"The village," he answered.

"There's been a lot of talk about the village lately. You wouldn't be the one they're all fussin' about, would you?" Ervin inquired.

"Just might be," Joshua acknowledged.

"Read about you in the papers. You got a lot of spunk, son, if I must say. Wish you luck in what you're trying to do. It's been a long-drawn-out battle here for years. It's not going to end easy."

Joshua just listened without commenting.

The fire was getting hot. Ervin took a good-sized fish from the catch hanging off the back of the boat, brought it over to a flat rock, cut it open, and filleted it. It was a good fish, almost sixteen inches long, meaty and tender. Taking a little grate from a box, Ervin rested it on two rows of stones neatly placed on either side of the fire, then placed the two halves of the fish on the grate and waited for them to roast.

George busied himself with the other things they needed for the meal—a big loaf of homemade bread, which he took from the picnic box, paper plates, three bottles of beer, and some clean cloths for napkins.

The aroma of roasting fish and salt air whet the appetites of the three men and made the meal even more delectable. The men ate heartily, chatting, laughing, enjoying their picnic at the seashore. They were friendly men from a village miles away. Their boat had drifted down shore when the wind had risen. They had a good time making the best of it, and their generous catch of fish would cheer their ride back home.

When they had finished the men packed their gear, said good-bye to Joshua, and shoved off. Joshua started up the rocks on his way back to the village.

CHAPTER 29

J OSHUA had hardly reached
the village square when the sky turned black and ominous.
A severe storm was imminent. Joshua picked up his pace
and walked in the direction of Downers Road. Father
Donnelly had invited him to stay at the parish house on
occasions like this. No sooner had he reached the house
when all the heavens broke loose. The rain came in
torrents. Joshua thought of the men who were on their
way back home from fishing. They lived up the coast. It
was over an hour and a half ago since they had left. They
should have made it home in plenty of time. At worst they
were close to home, which was a fishing village, and there
would be motorboats in the vicinity that could come to
their aid.

Marie answered the door, surprised to see Joshua. Her
face lighted up. "Hurry inside," she said, "before you get
drenched. Your timing was perfect. One minute later and
you would have been soaked."

Joshua went inside. Marie took him into the living
room and called the pastor, who came down immediately.

"What a pleasant surprise!" the priest said.

"I decided to take you up on your offer," Joshua said.
"That sure is some storm, and it doesn't look like it's going
to let up anytime soon."

"No, it doesn't. Well, I can't say I'm unhappy it's raining, if that is what it takes to get you to come stay here at the house. Where are you coming from? You're all wet with perspiration."

"I've just walked back across the meadow from the sea. I took a walk out there to collect my thoughts and rest awhile. As I was about to leave two men who had been fishing pulled their boat to shore and offered to share their meal with me. It was kind of them. When we finished I walked back here. It was an enjoyable walk and a perfect day for it."

It was close to six o'clock. The priest was just finishing his office work for the day and would be able to spend time with his friend. He had hoped he would come and spend more time than he usually did.

"Joshua, you know where your room is," Elmer told his guest matter-of-factly. "There are towels and whatever else you need in the closet. Make yourself at home. If you want to take a little rest, you're welcome to it. I'll be in my room if you'd like to come in and chat awhile before supper. We won't be eating until eight o'clock. By then you should have worked up a good appetite. I'm going to have a little drink around seven if you want to wait until then. It's up to you. I want you to feel completely at home."

"I'll just wash up," Joshua responded, "and rest for a few minutes. Then I'll be in better shape to socialize."

"Whatever. I'll be in my room."

Joshua went upstairs and the priest went into the kitchen to tell Marie they'd be having a guest for supper.

———

The priest's bedroom was not too artfully decorated. An old brass bed that his mother had left him dominated the room. An antique dresser and a highboy, both of these pieces inherited, filled what little space there was left. A simple crucifix hung on the wall behind the bed. On the wall across from the bed was a picture of the mother of Jesus. In the corner between two windows was an armchair.

The room adjacent was the pastor's private sitting room. It was nicely furnished and a source of pride to the old priest, who loved to entertain his fellow priests and throw card parties for them at least once or twice a month. The men enjoyed coming to his place because it was so relaxing, the food so plentiful and well prepared, and the furniture so comfortable.

After washing and resting for a short while, Joshua went to the pastor's room. Elmer offered him a seat and the two men plunged into immediate conversation. There were a lot of things to talk about. Before they got serious, however, Joshua asked the priest about his family, where he was from, where his family lived now, and if he got many occasions to visit with them. The priest went into minute detail in relating many memories of his parents, how they instilled in him at a tender age a deep love of Jesus and his mother, which had been the source of his strength all his life. He had three brothers and two sisters. Two brothers were dead, the other living in another part of the country. Both sisters had moved to another country with their husbands. They came back to visit occasionally, but not often enough. He really missed them and hoped, someday, to surprise them with a visit.

Then it was the priest's turn.

"Joshua, you really are a mystery. For some reason I

don't expect you will tell me where you are from, and for reasons I'm beginning to suspect, just like the Muslim man, Anwar. He was in to see me again the other day and asked if I had a book about Jesus' teachings. He wanted to compare them to the things he hears you teaching. He's quite taken up with you, as I'm sure you're aware."

The priest got lost in his own meandering and, to Joshua's comfort, forgot all the things he had intended to ask him. As it was seven o'clock, it was time for Elmer to release the creature and have their cocktail hour. He opened his well-stocked liquor cabinet and asked Joshua, "Well, young man, what will be your pleasure? I pride myself on having almost anything my guests enjoy."

"I think I'd like a sherry, dry, if you have it," Joshua responded.

"I sure do," the priest said with pride, taking out an unopened bottle of imported dry sherry.

After serving his guest the priest poured his own, a single shot of local whiskey with a little water. "I can't drink much anymore. I used to be able to have a couple before supper, but now if I take one, it is all I can handle. So I enjoy the one just as much as I used to enjoy two.

"Joshua, I have come to appreciate more and more what you have been doing in our village the past couple of months. It isn't just your working with the children. That's only part of it. It's the way you are, your personality, your ideas. You seem to be the very essence of the Gospels themselves, which I have been trying, in my own simple way these many years, to instill in the lives of the people. You are the epitome of everything I have tried to teach, and to meet this ideal so perfectly in you has touched my life almost miraculously. Your very presence has made my own faith come to life. For the first time I am not afraid to die and meet God. I feel in some strange way I have already met him, and I wasn't afraid. It brought me peace and not terror."

Joshua was touched by what the old priest said. For this good priest to have spent his whole life working for God and then to be frightened at the prospect of meeting Him didn't make sense.

"Elmer," Joshua said, "that is what people have done to religion. It is not what God wanted. Religious teachers so often miss the point of religion and dishonor God by teaching a God who is merciless and calculating and vindictive, which fills people with unbearable guilt that makes them afraid of God. That is not what God wanted. Jesus tried so hard to help people understand that God loves them as they are. He knows they are human. He made them that way and it is human to be weak and imperfect. God did not intend to make humans little gods. He created each individual to do a little job, to make their little contribution to help others and perfect his creation, and gave to each just what he or she needs to do that job. The rest of the personality is imperfect, but that's all right. The person will grow to become, in God's good time, what He wants that person to become. As long as people love God and care for others, they need never be afraid of meeting God."

"I understand now. I have met you and I am not afraid," the old priest said, not fully realizing the meaning of what he had said. Joshua smiled.

"That is the way the Church has taught religion for centuries, and it is hard to break from that mold," Elmer went on to say.

"Yes, that is unfortunate. The Church has assumed the role of Christ's stand-in, but has picked only the aspects of Christ's life that appealed to their need for power. The Church is the extension of Jesus' life in the world, but if it is to be effective, it must model itself on the way Jesus lived. Nobody was afraid of Jesus when he came to earth. They followed him everywhere because they knew he understood their anguish and their pain and looked past their failings. Sinners felt comforted in the presence of Jesus, and their lives changed in time. People don't feel comfortable with the Church because it has chosen to model itself on a legalistic, judgmental Christ molded in its own image. That frightens the sheep and drives them away and makes them afraid of God. The Church was intended to be the medium of Jesus' message, but instead it has become the message, and the living Jesus got lost."

It was time for supper. Marie called upstairs, telling the pastor everything was ready if they would like to come down.

The meal was simple. The old priest's diet had become more austere as he got older. Joshua wasn't too hungry, but enjoyed sharing a meal with his friends. When they began the meal, after they had said grace, Joshua took a piece of homemade bread, said a little prayer, broke the bread, and gave a piece to Elmer and one to Marie.

During supper the rain had stopped. Joshua and Elmer went outside to take a walk to the end of the village. The clean, newly washed atmosphere gave rise to a golden sunset. The two men stood on the roadside in silence, drinking in the changing colors of the sky reflecting across the meadow. The day had been a busy one. It ended well.

CHAPTER 30

SATURDAY came fast. Joshua spent the morning helping Charlie in the blacksmith shop. A few orders needed by farmers could not wait until Monday. Joshua was glad to help and had lunch with Charlie afterward.

That afternoon Joshua stayed out in the meadow carving little things out of wood, which he did often when there were lulls in his rather relaxed routine.

When early evening came Tim and Stella McGirr met Joshua at a crossroad in the meadow on their way to the Arab family's home for dinner so the three went together.

"You sure have changed things in the short time you've been here," Tim exclaimed to Joshua. "Who'd ever have dreamed I'd be going to an Arab's house for dinner? It was Father Donnelly who introduced me to them and we've become good friends."

"They are good people," Joshua remarked. "I think you will make good friends."

"Did you really heal their little boy of blindness?" Stella asked Joshua.

"It is faith that heals," Joshua answered. "The boy's family has deep faith, and it was rewarded by God."

"You know, Joshua," Tim said as they walked along the path, "people are beginning to develop strange ideas about you, like who you really are. I'm even beginning to wonder."

"People are so used to seeing meanness and pettiness that when a person acts normal and kind and caring, it is a shock and people begin to wonder. Why should what I do cause wonderment? Could anything be as simple as what I do?"

Tim wasn't talking about Joshua's life-style. He was asking about the extraordinary things that Joshua could do with such simplicity. Tim was too shrewd to shadowbox with Joshua. He'd wait until they were relaxed at dinner, then he'd press his point, when the others could come to his aid.

When they arrived Acmet answered the door. This time he was a perfect little gentleman, welcoming everyone and escorting them into the house, then announcing the guests' arrival to his family. Anwar and Miriam were most gracious in expressing their pleasure and immediately took them into the family room, where the rest of the family was relaxing. Everyone stood up and welcomed the guests when they came in. Then they all sat down to relax and enjoy refreshments before dinner.

A few minutes later Acmet's friend Peter came with his father and mother. They were all introduced and joined in the party. Peter's father, Jerry, was a comedian. He and Tim had been friends for years, and when the two got together they could entertain all night long. Peter's mother, Ann, was quiet, and said very little.

The dining room was splendid, with the vast table in the center of the room capable of seating almost twenty people. Costly accoutrements, some practical, some ornamental, filled the room. A large oil painting of a Middle East mountain village scene hung on the wall on the long side of the room. On the table, covered with beautiful linen, were expensive place settings, including sterling silverware. Two large platters of roast lamb rested on either side of the center of the table. Next to them were large dishes heaped high with saffron rice, boiled then fried so the children could have the chunks of crisp brown pieces scraped from the bottom of the pan.

Miriam seated each one strategically for the purpose of better conversation during the meal. Joshua she seated on her husband's right, with herself across from him. The others were scattered between members of her family.

Anwar offered to say a prayer before the meal. Everyone bowed his head. "Father in heaven, we have so much to be grateful for this evening. We have our health and our son whole again. We have the blessing of friends, new friends, who have given us so much love and companionship during this difficult time in our lives. You have given us Joshua, who has been a blessing to all of us, and who, by the beauty and simplicity of his life, has reflected into our lives the true presence of God and brought a new dimension to our own vision of life. We ask you to bless us all and to bless this food, which we gladly share in your honor. Finally, we ask you to bless this land with your peace," to which everyone responded with a hearty "Amen."

The children immediately asked if they could have the crispy rice from the bottom of the pan. Miriam said they would have to wait until the adults were served. The children knew that already, but it was their way of alerting the grown-ups that the crispy chunks were already spoken for so none of them would dare take those pieces, even if they were offered.

When everyone was served and the wine poured, the

conversation picked up in earnest and before long the whole room was buzzing like a beehive. The room was large enough, and the table vast enough, for several conversations to be carried on at the same time. Anwar told Joshua about his talks with Father Donnelly and that he shared the priest's views about his work with the children, and also of his awareness of Joshua's striking resemblance to the man in the Gospels. Joshua just kept eating, saying nothing.

"Joshua," Anwar said, "you are not even listening."

"Yes, I am," Joshua returned. "I have heard everything you have said. I am at a loss as to what to say to you."

"How did you ever arrive at such a close similarity to Jesus? The coincidence is remarkable."

At that point all the other converations stopped. Everyone turned toward Joshua.

"I wasn't aware," Joshua replied playfully, unwilling to let himself become the center of the conversation or to allow it to move along those lines.

"Come, my friend," Anwar persisted, "you are so much like him, it can't be by coincidence. It is either the result of years of imitation, which would certainly make you aware, or if you are unaware, then there is only one other possibility."

The man was sharp, and just as persistent to push his point as Joshua was to avoid it.

Joshua smiled, and then, to end the questioning, remarked simply, "We are all blessed to have the presence of God here in our midst this evening. May it be a true source of blessing to all of us, and may our lives be different from this day onward."

It was ambiguous, but it was not ambiguous to Anwar.

It was the only way Joshua could respond. Anwar had the assurance he needed, and his life from that moment would radically change. He and his wife looked at each other knowingly and thoughtfully. It took awhile for the conversations to pick up after that. Everyone was digesting what Joshua had just said, each understanding it in his own way.

Tim asked Anwar what life was like back in his own country.

"Not much different from here. People don't vary much. At home you have the very rich and the very poor. If you are industrious, you can better your lot. Our family used to live in tents not too many years ago. My grandfather, Elie, was shrewd and started a small business, importing at first little items, then slowly developing his business into a big operation. With the troubles in the country it's hard to know who are your friends and who are your enemies. There is a lot of hatred in our country, just like here. The message of Jesus to forgive endlessly has never been a part of our culture. By the way, Joshua, not to change the subject, but maybe you can explain that to me. I am having a very difficult time with Jesus' injunction to forgive. Peter thought he was being generous in offering to forgive seven times, and Jesus said, 'No, not seven times, but seventy times seven times.' Don't you think that's a bit much?"

Joshua sat back, looked around at everyone, and very seriously said, "What Jesus was trying to do was not to issue an impossible commandment, but to offer the key to true inner peace. He came to bring peace to troubled souls and to show people how to live in a way that would not only lead them to God, but help them find a meaning to life that made sense. He was deeply concerned about people's inability to find peace. His secret, which he lived himself, was in forgiveness, a forgiveness so complete that it never even allowed itself to take offense. And that is the key to peace, personal peace and peace among peoples—do not allow yourself to take offense. Always try to understand why people say and do the things they do, the inner anguish that gives rise to those things, and then it is hard to take offense. Indeed, you can even pity them. You may be wary, so you can protect yourself, but you can still reach out and be a brother and sister to those people, never despairing of trying to heal their troubled, tortured souls. Jesus himself lived that way. He never took offense, and his last words were 'Father, forgive them, they know not what they have done.' "

"How beautiful!" Anwar said. "That does make sense—and for the first time."

The rest of the evening was much more lighthearted, with Jerry and Tim providing the entertainment, keeping everyone laughing until almost midnight. Even Acmet's grandmother enjoyed them, though she couldn't understand everything they said.

The party ending, everyone left. Anwar insisted Joshua again stay for the night. He accepted. Although it was a social evening, lives were deeply affected that night, and no one there would ever be the same.

CHAPTER 31

FAR from the village, in another part of the country, six men were meeting in a dingy, poorly lighted, smoke-filled tavern. One of the men was Father Jack Brown, dressed in jeans and a turtleneck pullover. The others were leaders in their subversive organization. The purpose of the meeting was to discuss the bishops' pastoral letter and what should be their organization's response to the bizarre turn of events caused by the meddlesome stranger in the village where all this activity had originated.

The group admitted that the move to organize the children was shrewd and could be severely damaging to their organization's plans, but not necessarily fatal if they countered with the right moves.

"We certainly can't go after the bishops," one remarked. No one disagreed.

"We definitely can't touch the children," another commented.

"However," a man with coarse, cynical features suggested, "we might do something that would frighten the kids, intimidate them, and then cause their parents to forbid any further involvement."

That suggestion seemed to have potential and was worth pursuing. They discussed various possibilities, one

even recommending kidnapping some of the children.
That was rejected because it would turn their own people
against them. Finally, after much discussion, it was
decided to observe a total hands-off policy when it came to
the children. It could only backfire and arouse not just
local but international repercussions.

Inevitably, the focus came around to Joshua. Who the
hell is he anyway? He is, after all, only a stranger. No one
has any ties to him, no personal loyalties, no attachment.
The priest suggested they center their action against him.
He was the one who started the whole thing. If they did
something to him, there might be a stir for a while, but
having no roots here, he would soon be forgotten. The
children, having been deprived of their leader, would
disband and forget the whole undertaking.

The suggestion appealed to everyone, but what action
they should take was an issue not too easily resolved. One
suggested roughing up Joshua but decided against that as
being unproductive and something that would arouse the
sympathy of the people. Besides, the media would use it to
maximum advantage, making him even more of a hero.
And he would still be around.

After a long lull in the conversation, one man calmly
and slowly suggested, "Why not just eliminate him?"

"You mean really kill him?" another questioned,
shocked.

"Yes, why not?" the man said coldly.

The priest, taken aback by the turn the conversation
had taken, tried to make the point that it might not be the
practical thing to do. "After all," he said, "the fellow isn't
really evil and he means well."

The others jumped in immediately. "Hell, what do you
mean, he means well? He's been out to destroy everything

we've broken our backs over all our lives trying to accomplish," one man objected, to which the others agreed. The priest made a few other feeble objections but was overruled each time.

By the end of the evening they had all come to an agreement that Joshua had to be eliminated. As strongly opposed as he was to this solution, the priest finally gave his consent. The only question remaining was how this would be carried out.

"The fellow meets with the kids in the village square almost every day, though his schedule does vary," a man who lived in the village commented. "He almost always ends with them at noon, again in the square. So what we do should be done at that time." They all agreed to that—the action would take place in the village square at noon.

The next question to be settled was just what should be done. At that point a thin, wiry man said bluntly, "I think we should have one of our men from the village do the job. Two of them are excellent marksmen and would be better able to plan the details. No one would suspect them, seeing them around. If whoever does it uses a silencer, no one will realize what has happened. This will make for an easy getaway in the midst of the confusion."

"Good idea!" another man said.

The group had no problem with that suggestion. It was accepted. They knew just the one for it. That was also decided without delay. Whoever did it would have to make his own arrangements as to the details. They would contact him the next morning.

With all that business agreed upon, the group broke up in the early hours of the morning, not much after sunrise.

In another part of the country, on the following night, a similar meeting took place in the comfortable surroundings of a parish house. It was the house of the Reverend John V. Maislin. He had gathered the leaders of his pious hatemongers to determine what had to be done to end the farce of the busybody stranger in the village and stanch the flow of goodwill that was poisoning the atmosphere all across the country.

The scenario was much the same as the meeting the previous night, the suggestions similar, the objections parallel, and the conclusions identical. After all, there were few options available to counter an epidemic of goodness. Joshua had to be eliminated. The practical way was to assign a member living in the village to do the job. By eliminating him the cause of the problem would be eradicated, and the children would be panicked into abandoning the movement. Like the other group, they had to ascertain the daily movements of Joshua and determine when he would be in the village square. That was the only constant in his daily schedule, his appearance in the square when he finished talking with the children in the fields.

32

JOSHUA'S WORK went on uninterrupted each day, as if nothing was happening. His relaxed, serene manner showed no sign of anxiety or troubling worries. It wasn't that he was unaware. He was only too aware of just what was being planned, but such was his trust in his Father's closeness to him, he knew all would work the way his Father willed. So he faced each day unflinchingly.

After working with the children in the morning, he would help Charlie in the afternoon at the blacksmith shop. Charlie was almost caught up with his work, so he wouldn't be needing Joshua much longer. There was only one small change in Joshua's daily routine. He was staying longer in the fields with the children and not ending every day in the square. Only once or twice a week would he finish their gatherings in the square before sending them home for lunch. In the beginning Joe used to bring him lunch, but now the kids took turns, deciding among themselves who would bring his lunch the following day.

On the surface nothing really changed. Little things were happening that meant nothing to the children but whose significance Joshua understood only too well. A couple of children at different times would ask Joshua what he would be doing each day, and on following days, and if they would be ending their meetings in the square at noon. Joshua looked at the children with sadness in his eyes, troubled that calloused men would use innocent children as pawns in their dirty schemes, unconcerned that what they were setting up the children to do would scar them with guilt for life. Joshua was careful not to give the children any information, more for their own good than for his protection. The men would have to get their information elsewhere.

"Now run along, little ones," Joshua would say to them each time they came to question him, "and don't trouble yourselves with such things. Just be happy and be free and enjoy your play."

During the week a most unusual event began to take shape. A group of older kids organized an all-village soccer game, and rather than draw up teams from each side of town, they decided to divide the town down the middle so that each team would be half Protestant and half Catholic. When they told Joshua what they had done, and that the game was scheduled for the next week on Saturday, Joshua was overjoyed and proud over what these young people had done. They were also making a determined effort to encourage the whole town to come to the game. The game would be held on the field near the school. The kids personally went to the politicians and pressured them into coming, and although they all felt threatened politically if they attended, they ended up promising to come. The children even invited the police and the local contingent of soldiers that patrolled the area. No one could believe what was happening.

Each day the teams practiced diligently, each determined to win this unique and historic game. Naturally, Joshua was given a special invitation. He enjoyed seeing the young people planning and playing together and having a good time. It made him realize his movement now was irreversible. Once the children found each other in this way and with this depth of intimacy, and were fired, as they were, by an ideal they all cherished, Joshua knew it would not end and would survive well into the children's adult lives. He felt a deep sense of peace and satisfaction that a goal dreamed about for so many years for such basically good people was finally on the verge of fulfillment. All it needed was a catalyst to generate a chain reaction so that what was happening in the village would spread all across the country.

Joshua's meetings with the children were held each day as usual. In the afternoon they watched the soccer teams practice. All the kids were caught up in the excitement. Even the parents picked up the children's enthusiasm.

By the time Saturday came the whole town was fired up and couldn't wait for the game to start. The field was packed. Even old folks and crippled people came. The clergy met on the way to the field and, in a heartwarming expression of solidarity and genuine friendship, stayed together during the game. Truly a miracle had been wrought, and, more than that, another miracle when the politicians showed up. They really had little choice. Everyone else in town was there. Their absence would have branded them. Townsfolk who had been at odds for years came walking out to the field together. Their children had become close friends, and the parents rather sheepishly found themselves socializing.

By two o'clock, starting time, the field was filled to capacity. The two teams, each named after its side of town, the Westside Tigers and the Eastside Rangers, came running onto the field to the loud applause of everyone, the little kids screaming, calling their friends' names.

The whistle blew. The Tigers brought the ball deep into Rangers' territory. One of the Rangers hit the ball with his head, driving it back across the center line into an open space. Another Ranger contacted and by good teamwork brought the ball almost to the goal, when a Tiger ran up behind him and broke the advance. The ball went back and forth furiously, cheered on by the excitement of the crowd as they shouted their support of their team.

It was almost fifteen minutes into the game when a Tiger kicked the ball from the right and drove it clear past the goalie. The Tiger fans went wild. It was a Protestant boy who made the goal. His teammates were beside themselves, the Catholic kids hugging him, which was touching for all the grown-ups to witness. Joshua clapped too. The people near him were wondering which side he was on. He applauded both teams when they did well.

By halftime the score was Tigers three, Rangers two. It was a hot day, the sun beating down fiercely. The kids kept wiping their faces, trying desperately to keep dry.

The second half was even more exciting than the first half. The Rangers tied the game shortly after the half began and held the tie for a good part of the period, until a teammate fumbled the ball only a few feet from his own goal when a fast-moving Tiger slammed it into the goal.

Soon after the game had started five strangers had appeared at the game, mingling with the crowd. They did not, however, come unnoticed. Elmer spotted them walking down from the road and immediately recognized them. He poked Russ and pointed them out. Russ turned and looked, but didn't have the slightest idea as to their identity or the significance of their presence.

"Don't you know who they are?" Elmer asked, surprised.

"No," Russ answered, "I don't have the slightest idea."

"They are officers in the radical Catholic underground, though I doubt if anyone around here would know them. I had a chance meeting with them years ago at a social affair and they were pointed out to me. I'll never forget them, though I doubt if they would remember me."

Word of the plot to assassinate Joshua had leaked out from the splinter groups that had planned it to the officials of the main underground organization, who were furious when they heard of it, furious that such a small outfit would dare do something with such shocking reverberations. These men had come down to the village on an intelligence mission to see firsthand just what was transpiring in the village and report back to the council.

People standing near them, knowing they were strangers, strained their ears to pick up pieces of their conversation. One of those townsfolk was Tim McGirr, and what he picked up was shocking. He couldn't wait until the game was over so he could tell his pastor what he had heard.

In the meantime, the game was moving fast. Two more goals were made by both sides by the middle of the second half, and the score, four minutes before the final whistle, was five to four. Every now and then Elmer would look furtively over at the strangers. Oddly enough, they had become interested in the game and found themselves taking sides, at times applauding a good play. Elmer noticed Tim standing in the crowd near them and was hoping he was discreetly eavesdropping.

With two minutes left, the Rangers scored another goal, tying the game. The roar of the small crowd was gigantic, louder than seemed possible for its size, the people's excitement spurring on the players to final heroic efforts to win the game for their team.

In the last thirty seconds the Rangers' youngest player, a boy by the name of Jay, who had not played all during the game, and who was put in at the last minute out of sympathy, was standing near the goal. A hard-driven ball struck him in the chest and landed practically at his feet. Half not realizing what he was doing, he kicked it. The ball went flying past the goalie and hit the post at an angle, then shot into the goal. The Rangers won. The whole crowd went wild. Teammates hugged Jay. He would be the hero for a long time. People ran out onto the field, mobbing their favorite players.

After a few minutes both teams worked their way together, forming a wedge, and moved through the crowd to where Joshua was standing by himself, watching all the fun the people were having. The kids had decided beforehand to do what they were doing no matter who won the game. They surrounded Joshua, picking him up and carrying him on their shoulders across the field. All the villagers clapped and shouted their joy and gratitude to this simple, unassuming stranger who had made this whole miracle possible.

The five strangers left the field shaken and confused, profoundly affected by what they had just experienced. Never had anyone dreamed that what was taking place would even be possible, and yet they were seeing it with their own incredulous eyes. And they could also see the imminent possibility for the fulfillment of their cherished dreams of peace in their land.

The game over, the people dispersed, going to their homes to celebrate. Some of the men went to the tavern to celebrate before going home. Tim was one of them. The clergy met at Elmer's. Since he was the oldest clergyman in town, he had invited them all to his place for a party. They picked up Joshua as they were walking across the field and insisted he come with them to celebrate. He good-naturedly went along with them, happy to celebrate the joyous occasion.

The players on both teams went to their homes to wash up and prepare for parties with their families and teammates. It was a totally triumphant day for the children. It made no difference who won the game. Their real triumph was a much loftier goal. They were now keenly conscious of their power to bring about radical change. Their lives would never again be the same. Joshua's work was done, indeed, well done, thorough to the last detail, showing the exquisite finesse of God's personal touch.

Elmer collared Tim on his way to the tavern and took him aside. "Tim," Elmer started by saying, "I noticed those fellows near you during the game. Did you overhear anything?"

"Did I overhear anything?" Tim responded, startled, sensing the priest knew something he didn't. He was now curious himself and decided to bargain with the foxy old pastor.

"Who are they, anyway?" Tim asked.

"Tell me what you heard first, then I'll tell you who they are," Elmer retorted, a little impatient at being trapped by his own move.

"Well, they didn't have much to say at first," Tim said, "but after a while they began to open up. One of the fellows made the remark 'You know, I can't believe what I'm seeing here today. I have to admit, I'm impressed. If this spreads, it could change the face of the whole country.' One of the others agreed. A third man added, 'Yes, and for the better. The bloody devils who are plotting to destroy it must be really sick. This stranger has accomplished single-handedly what we have been unable to bring about with all our efforts. Why would anyone want to destroy what is being done here? What I see here I've dreamed of all my life.'

"Only one fellow didn't seem to agree completely with the others," Tim continued, "but, you have to remember, what I'm saying is not exactly what they said. They were careful. I'm piecing together bits of the conversation, trying to give it to you in a way that makes sense. This other fellow had his doubts as to whether something like this could last, given the many years of hatred that have transpired. But even he admitted he was impressed. I couldn't help but wonder what they were talking about when they mentioned someone trying to destroy it all. What do you think they were talking about, Father?"

"I don't know," Elmer answered. "I'd give anything to find out."

"Father, you said you'd tell me who they were. Who were they, anyway?" Tim asked, his curiosity piqued.

"Tim," the priest confided to him, "they are officers in the organization. I suspect they must have gotten wind of something afoot and were sent to see things here for themselves and report back so the council could plan a response. The fellows you saw have a reputation in the group for being moderate and level-headed. They were sent for intelligence purposes, I'm sure. But I would like to know what's up."

"I can't imagine any rational person finding fault with what's taking place here," Tim said.

The priest agreed, but then commented, "There are

some people who are so filled with hate that they can't tolerate goodness. It takes away their excuse to hate, and of necessity they have to see evil in innocence. . . ."

The priest prudently ended his thoughts at that point, not thinking it wise to say any more. But he was thinking about that radical priest who had his followers in the town, as well as others who had a reputation for being borderline cases.

"All we can do is pray," the priest ended by saying. The two men then parted, Tim going to the tavern, the priest catching up with the other clergy, who were waiting for him.

The whole village celebrated that night, not the victory of the Rangers, but the victory that filled everyone's heart with a peace and joy that could come only from God. Even the Muslim family, who had been at the game with everyone else, celebrated, inviting Jerry and Ann and Pete to their house for a party. Seeing the miracle that had taken place almost overnight, Anwar had decided to take his family back to their country in the Middle East and try to do the same thing in their family's village that Joshua had been able to accomplish in this village. He would discuss the matter with Joshua and seek his advice and his prayers.

33

THE FIVE STRANGERS at
the soccer game reported back that very evening to their
council. The consensus of the five was that Joshua was a
simple, but obviously a very extraordinary, person to have
managed to weld that whole village together into a totally
transformed people. The men described the eerie sense of
a presence at the game that was beyond anything human,
but couldn't put their finger on what was responsible for
it. They themselves felt the peace that the people in the
village had come to know, and they could understand why
everyone was so completely loyal to the man they called
Joshua.

"Maybe the bishops are right for once," one of the men
said. "Something has indeed happened to that village, and
if it does spread, it can create the atmosphere we need to
really effect the kind of change that will make sense and
benefit everyone."

Another jumped in immediately. "But we have to find
out what those bloody fools are plotting or everything will
be just talk. They could destroy whatever good might come
from this. Without realizing it, this fellow Joshua has set
up everything we need to accomplish our own goals if we
play it cool and plot our own strategy well."

The chairman asked if anyone had any more details on

the plot. No one could offer anything. Their contacts were vague.

It was decided before the meeting ended to assign discreet individuals to ferret out exact details of the plot to assassinate Joshua and to use whatever means necessary to prevent it from happening. Whether it could be prevented depended upon the ability of the agents to pump enough information from their sources to be able to piece together the time, date, and the individuals involved. What the group did not know was that there were two distinct plots planned by two different groups. It would be almost two days later before they obtained that information. They needed to develop all new contacts to track down intelligence concerning the second group. With the uncanny and efficient network these men had, it was entirely possible for them to accomplish the task, given enough time. The problem was, they didn't have much time.

Both groups involved in the plots were well along in the planning of final details. They had both pinpointed the dates on which Joshua would be in the village square at noontime—only two days of the next week, Wednesday and Friday. They both separately decided that Wednesday would be too soon to get everything ready but that day could be used as a dress rehearsal, at least to determine Joshua's position in the square, how long he stayed at the spot before dismissing the children, the best vantage points, and the easiest and quickest escape routes with the least chance of detection.

That Sunday morning Joshua went to the Presbyterian church for the service. He could and did go to Elmer's church frequently because he had Mass every morning.

The other churches had services only on Sunday, so he was limited as to when he could attend.

Russ was surprised to spot him in the back of the church. His sermon that day was on "Life as a Soccer Game." Joshua smiled a number of times at the clever way he took things that happened at the game the day before and applied them to the people's everyday life, and showed how beautiful life could be if everyone realized how much we all needed one another. He said that it is not how much we have done for ourselves that God will one day ask us, or the amount that we have accumulated for ourselves, but what we have done to better our brothers' lot and how much of the gifts God has given to us we have been willing to share with our hurting brothers and sisters that will concern God. "We have all made terrible mistakes by being afraid of our Catholic brothers and sisters and cutting them out of our social and political and economic life, making it all but impossible for them to live. Hopefully, the beautiful stranger in our midst has forever changed that by giving us a vision that can translate into a whole new life for all of us, a life that can make us all feel good inside, and make our prayers to our Father meaningful and sincere, and bring down upon us the rich blessing of our common Father."

Joshua was clearly pleased, and told Russ afterward when they were having breakfast together in the manse. It was at breakfast that Russ asked Joshua if he was aware of anything untoward taking place. Joshua said simply that he knew some people weren't too happy about what his work was accomplishing and would try to stop it, but that could not happen because it was his Father's will that this work should not fail. Joshua's definitiveness in answering this way preempted any further discussion on the matter.

He seemed to take every eventuality into consideration and discounted what seemed to others ominous and threatening.

Joshua spent the rest of Sunday with Russ and his wife. They had a relaxed, restful afternoon. For the evening they invited friends over for dinner and had a pleasant time just indulging in light talk and sharing stories about each of their lives. Joshua shared his insights into the personalities of some of the children who followed him faithfully.

At the end of the evening Russ invited Joshua to stay for the night, which he did.

Heavy clouds covered the sky all day Tuesday, but had passed by Wednesday. It turned out to be a beautiful day as Joshua met with the children in the meadow. They ended the morning by gathering in the square just before noon. Joe brought his trumpet and asked Joshua if he would really try to play well. He tried hard to teach him and felt bad that he hadn't succeeded. Joshua promised to take his playing seriously and took the trumpet from Joe. Putting it to his lips, he warmed up for a while and then started to play. What he played and the way he played shocked everyone. The kids sat there on the pavement in utter disbelief at the beautiful music that came forth from the instrument. He didn't play long, not more than two or three minutes, but the way he played brought tears to Joe's eyes and the eyes of many of the children as well. Joe's tears turned to a broad smile as he swelled with pride at having taught Joshua how to play the trumpet so beautifully.

When Joshua finished his face was flushed from the strenuous exercise. The kids clapped and applauded. Joshua smiled, thanked Joe for being such a good and patient teacher, and gave him back his trumpet. The kids all felt good that Joshua could play so well. They used to feel sorry for him.

"Joshua," Joe said, "I never dreamed you could play so well. I knew you were not playing seriously the other times, but this was beautiful."

Joshua just smiled.

It was a little after twelve when the group disbanded, going home for lunch. Joshua spent the afternoon at the coast, just thinking, praying silently, and gathering together his courage and strength for the crucial time ahead. He had supper that evening at the McGirrs and spent the night there, to everyone's great pleasure, especially Christopher's. The family was in rare good spirits. Even Joshua was lighthearted, playing cards with the kids and having a beer with Tim. When the children went to bed the adults sat on the front porch talking until late in the evening, when they all retired.

CHAPTER 34

T HURSDAY MORNING came.
A mist from the sea hung over the fields. Chris was the
first up, or thought he was. He wanted to spend time alone
with his friend before the others crowded him out, like
they usually did. To Chris's surprise Joshua was already
up, sitting on the front porch watching the animals across
the yard. A cock crowed, breaking the morning silence.
Other animals were slowly coming to life.

Chris stood there, saying nothing.

"Good morning, Christopher," Joshua said, motioning
for him to come and sit down next to him on the porch.

"See those fields, little one?" Joshua said. "One day
they will be filled with trees, good trees to support your
families and bring prosperity to your people. Ask your
daddy to plant little trees with you. It will be a job just for
you and him. When you are big they will be fully grown."

Chris said nothing, just listened and looked out across
the fields, imagining a forest filling the meadow, something
he had never seen. He liked the idea.

Joshua knew how hard it was for the boy to get his
father's attention, and this would give him a chance to
spend hours with his father all by himself as they planted
the trees. Christopher looked forward to the project with
excitement.

After a few minutes the house was buzzing with activity, with kids getting dressed and running about doing their chores in the barn, feeding the chickens and the other animals.

Stella was busy getting breakfast ready, the daily feast the whole family heartily enjoyed.

After breakfast Joshua prayed a blessing over everyone, hugged them all, then he and Tim left, walking across the fields together, Tim on his way to work, Joshua about his daily work.

"Joshua," Tim said as they walked along, "Chris told me about the tree project you have planned for the two of us. Although I can't help but feel I'm being conned, I like the idea. Why didn't someone do it years ago? It could have brought much needed income to our family. Chris will have fun working with me. He's forever trying to take me aside to do things with him, but I rarely have the time. I suppose I could come right home from work and spend the time with him before supper. It would be good for both of us to work on a project like that. I may not live to benefit from it, but the kids will reap the benefits long after I'm gone, and that's what counts. Yes, I think that's probably a good idea. Thanks."

"Your people have given much to humanity," Joshua said to Tim, "even to those who have tried so hard to destroy them and their loyalty to God. But nothing passes my Father unnoticed. It is now time for you to rebuild yourselves as a people. You have the resources. Use them."

"You do a lot of thinking, don't you?" Tim said to Joshua, then added, "The men at the plant have been talking about you more and more. At first they thought you were an odd fellow, but lately they've come around to appreciate what you have done for us all. Our children are much happier than they've ever been. To see all the kids in the village playing together, and even the grown-ups beginning to socialize, is truly a remarkable accomplishment. It is even affecting the atmosphere at work. Two Catholics were given promotions at the plant. That's been unheard of, and I mean big promotions, and the Protestants congratulated them, another first. It's all because of you, Joshua. I hope you realize that."

Joshua said nothing, just kept walking, a tear trickling down his cheek.

At the square the two men parted, Tim going to his job and Joshua down the street to Elmer's church. Men and women passing him along the way greeted him warmly.

The priest was in his garden as usual, praying his morning prayers.

"Just in time again, my friend," the priest said to Joshua as he approached. "I'm just saying the last two Psalms. Want to join me?"

"Yes, I would," Joshua replied.

"I'm sure you know them by heart," Elmer said playfully.

Joshua smiled. The priest intoned the psalm "The Lord is my shepherd, there is nothing I shall want. He makes me to lie down in green pastures."

Joshua picked up the second verse of the Twenty-third Psalm: "He leads me beside still waters, and refreshes my soul.

He leads me in right paths for his name's sake.

Though I should walk in the valley of the shadow of death, I will fear no evil, for you are with me.

Your rod and your staff, they give me comfort.

. . . I will soon again dwell in the house of the Lord forever."

The psalm was apropos to the turn of events in Joshua's life, and the words fit perfectly.

The two men finished the prayers and went into the church for the breaking of bread, as the early Christians used to call the Mass.

Joshua sat in the back of the church, as he usually did, absorbed in his thoughts, resting in his Father's presence.

After Mass the two men went into the rectory for breakfast. Marie beamed when she saw Joshua walking in the door.

"Joshua," Elmer said as soon as they sat down, "you look calm and peaceful as usual. I assume everything is going well?"

Joshua knew the old priest was prying, but he was also concerned.

"Yes, everything is right on schedule according to plan," Joshua said simply.

The priest couldn't understand Joshua's calmness. He himself was anxious by nature and Joshua's serenity in the face of brewing storms totally baffled him.

"I have heard some things that worry me, and I can't help but be afraid for you. There were some strangers in town at the soccer game last Saturday. I know who they are and I can't help but be troubled as to their intentions. They have been involved in underground activities for years, and I'm sure their coming here has something to do with you. Tim McGirr was standing near them and overheard them discussing a plot involving the village."

"Father, don't worry yourself. Nothing will happen to the children. My Father's will is being accomplished exactly according to his plans. I know you are concerned. When events come to pass do not judge by appearances. Things are not what they appear. It is not the same as before. This is to teach the world a lesson in how far their hatred has taken them. Do not be troubled."

Joshua said all this to allay the fears of the old priest who had come to love him so deeply. There was no way, however, for him to understand then what Joshua was talking about, but it would be clear when it did come to pass.

Joshua stayed at the rectory a little longer than usual and was there when Anwar came to visit the priest. He was surprised to see Joshua and glad he was there. He had wanted to tell Joshua how meeting him had changed his whole life.

"Joshua," Anwar said to him, "I can't tell you what you have done for me. My life is completely changed. I see God differently. I see people, no matter who they are, or what they believe, as God's dearly loved children. I see the life of each human being as a sacred creation of God, to be loved and respected, and never, for whatever motives, to be desecrated. And to atone for the terrible things of the past, I am going back to my own country and work with the children there, the way you have here, to teach them to build a better life for the future. It is the first time in my life that I feel I have a purpose."

Joshua listened, and when Anwar finished he said very solemnly, "Anwar, the troubles there are not the same as here. They are much more complex. You must remember that and consider it when you plan your work. You must be very careful and pray each day. Let God guide your every step. You cannot do that work alone. You do not have the understanding. No human does, so listen to the gentle voice of God each step along the way. With your new faith and your new direction, your friends will be wary. Respect where each one is coming from. Do not try to change their beliefs. That's God's business. Just be a light in the darkness and a warm fire in a cold night. People will see your goodness and will come to see God's light shining through you. There will be those who hate goodness and will try to harm you, but do not be afraid. You and your family will be protected from above. No evil will touch you. Go there in peace."

Anwar was deeply touched by the prophetic insights of his gentle friend and reassured by his words. They were obviously from God. Although he was determined to go back home, he was burdened with fears about his family and their safety. Joshua's words had a profound effect on him, as if God himself were talking to him. He felt a strange calmness when Joshua had finished.

Father Donnelly was also impressed with what Joshua had said to Anwar, but said nothing.

Joshua excused himself, saying the children would be waiting for him. They all embraced and said good-bye. Joshua left. Anwar stayed to talk to the priest.

In the meantime, the men assigned by the underground council were frantically tring to track down leads in a last-minute attempt to frustrate the plots to assassinate Joshua. The only detail they could pin down was the date on which the plot would be carried out. The nature of the plot and the exact time were still unknown. They continued pursuing leads all day long. It wasn't until late Thursday morning that they found out the two plots were to be executed at the exact same time. What that time was they still had no idea.

While all this feverish activity was taking place, Joshua met with the children as if nothing was happening. There was no noticeable change in his manner. He joked with the children and was perhaps a little more affectionate and playful than on other days. Joe's Protestant friend played the trumpet as usual and did an excellent performance for a boy who had been taking lessons for such a short time. The children sang along with the guitar players, expressing the joy and exuberance that Joshua had brought into their lives. It was an unusually happy day, although it must have had a certain gloom for Joshua, knowing with his uncanny knowledge the dark events swirling all around him.

Pete and Acmet sat in the front of the group, right near Joshua. During a break Pete asked Joshua, "What is the matter?"

"Why do you think something is the matter, Peter?" Joshua asked him.

"Because I feel you are sad, and it makes me feel sad," the little boy replied.

"Don't you worry, Peter. God always takes care of us. We all have our work to do, and we must face each day bravely, knowing that God is always by our side. Even out of things that hurt he brings good. Never be afraid when you are doing God's work."

"I hear people talking," Peter said. The boy had an unbelievable ability to pick up information from people's casual, loose remarks and put things together. "I hear people talking and I can tell something is going to happen. Isn't it?"

"Whatever happens is part of God's plan, so we shouldn't worry. Much good will come from it. Hurt is only temporary. The good that comes from it is endless. Memories of good things and those who love us will always be precious. No one can take those from us. Always treasure those memories and share with others the beautiful things you have experienced, like you did with Acmet. Because you cared, God healed him. And remember, I will always love you and be with you."

"Joshua," Peter said, attempting to find out just what was wrong, "if something happens, will you leave us? And if you leave us, where will you go?"

"If something happens, little one, I will return to my Father," Joshua answered.

"Can I come with you?" the boy persisted.

"Not now," Joshua said, "but when your work is done you will come, so always be strong and be loyal to God's wishes."

"I will miss you if you go," Peter said with tears in his eyes.

"I will always be near you. When you talk to me I will be by your side and even in your heart," Joshua said, trying to console his little friend.

Acmet listened intently to the whole conversation and was himself feeling sad at what he had heard. Joshua looked at the two of them, took them in his arms and held them close, then told them to go and play and think happy thoughts.

After the break the children reassembled for a little story before being dismissed for the day. When they were all seated on the grass, Joshua began his story.

"A good and kind king had a vast kingdom. The people of the kingdom fought among themselves over who was the most favored of his subjects. In their jealousy they grew to hate and despise one another and even made laws to destroy each other. They went so far as to set up separate parts of the kingdom, forbidding each other to cross the others' boundaries. They taught their children also to hate one another. The king was badly distressed over all the hatred that poisoned his kingdom and destroyed the peace and joy he had so carefully planned for his subjects. The subjects had no idea how angry and sad the king was over all of them and the way they treated one another. The bitterness lasted for centuries, and not knowing what else to do, the king sent his son to visit the kingdom and heal the divisions.

"When the son came he was sad to see how terrible was the anger and meanness the people had for one another. The adults showed no willingness to heal the wounds, so the son decided to work among the children, especially when he saw how sad and lonely they were. He would bring them the peace their parents rejected. The son met with the children every day and taught them how to have fun together and care for one another.

"When evil men saw the children were beginning to love one another, they became angry because it was destroying hatred throughout the land and undermining their power and evil schemes, which could thrive only where there is hatred and suspicion. In their fury and spite over the son's goodness, they plotted to destroy him and the work he was doing. They tried but they could not harm him, because it was beyond their ability to touch him.

"When the children saw the terrible things those evil men tried to do to the son whom they had come to love, they were determined to carry on the son's work and make sure his mission to bring peace to the kingdom would succeed. They carried his message far beyond the boundaries hatred had built and they reached children everywhere.

"As time passed the children were able to do what for

centuries the grown-ups were unable to accomplish—to bring peace to the kingdom, because they had learned that to have peace there must first be love and caring for one another."

The children sat through the story spellbound. Joshua's calm, soothing voice added to the magic of his storytelling. When he finished they all clapped, though they had not fully realized the meaning of his story.

When the story ended Joshua dismissed the children and walked up Stonecastle Road to the hill overlooking the fields and just sat there for the longest time, absorbing the quiet and beauty of the landscape. He had finished his work with the blacksmith and wasn't needed there any-more, so he had the rest of the afternoon to himself, which he spent walking through both parts of town. He met the Wesleyan minister, a venerable old man, as he was taking his daily walk. They had a long talk as they walked through the village together. Joshua had been in his church on one or two occasions and had spoken with him briefly, but not having many people in his congregation, they were not very involved in the events that embroiled others.

After walking through the Protestant area Joshua wandered through the Catholic part of town, greeting people along the way, stopping to talk to old folks on their way to church for a visit or workingmen on their way home from work. Some of the children were playing along the way. He stopped to chat with them and moved on.

It was almost six o'clock when he went down to the Almost Home Tavern for supper. When he sat down some of the men came around the table to talk with him. They all knew him by now and enjoyed being in his company. They talked mostly about the soccer game and praised

Joshua for the job he had done with the kids. When the waiter came with his supper the men were polite enough to let him eat in peace. After finishing he spent a few minutes with them, talking to them at the bar and encouraging them to continue the beautiful work the children had started. The men felt things would be different from now on, since everyone had finally found each other. Joshua left and went out into the meadow, lighted a fire because it was chilly, and spent a good part of the night absorbed in prayer.

CHAPTER 35

FRIDAY MORNING came with
a severe thunderstorm that passed through the meadow
near the coast but bypassed the village. It lasted only
fifteen or twenty minutes, then turned into a glorious,
sunny day, with a blue sky as light as silk and the air as
fresh as the first day of spring.

Joshua spent the morning walking through the meadow
thinking, feeling, and praying to his Father. He knew the
day would go well, but he was concerned for the children.
It would be a difficult day for them and he wanted
assurances that his Father would keep them in his care.
He had grown fond of these children who had been so
open, so accepting, and so willing to commit their young
lives to his mission.

It was late in the morning when all the children had
assembled in the meadow. The routine was the same as on
other mornings, and Joshua was the same as always. The
children took turns providing the entertainment for the
group.

At the same time, in the nearby city, members of the
underground council were meeting to discuss the latest
intelligence concerning the plot. They had found, after
working all night, that the two separate plots were to be
executed in the village itself. They still could not pinpoint

the times, though the men knew they had to take place some time on this day. It was crucial to find out immediately if they were going to be able to stop them. The chairman decided to dispatch a contingent to the village to survey the area and make whatever on-the-spot decisions were necessary to abort the plots. The others were to continue to check out leads.

After the children assembled in the meadow, Joshua met them on a little knoll that provided a view of the whole area. Everyone seemed in a lighthearted mood. It was such a beautiful day. How could they feel otherwise? A little before noon the children took their break. Joshua told them to reassemble in the square. After a few minutes of meeting with their friends and socializing, Joshua started toward the village. The children followed.

Arriving at the square first, Joshua sat on the wall and waited for the children to reassemble. Once they had all gathered and were seated on the pavement, Joshua stood up and began speaking to them in unusually tender language.

"Little ones, you are truly blessed by God. You have been chosen to do a special work for him. The grown-ups have grown weary and tired of the heavy burden of solving life's problems. A new way has to begin. You have been chosen by God to start on that way. You can see what your love and your caring has already accomplished in the village. You have been able to transform the whole community. Where before there was hatred and suspicion and fear, now there is love and friendship and trust. The secret is to love and never to take offense. Always try to understand the tortured anguish that drives people to do the mean things they do, and it will not be hard to forgive. Let your love conquer all obstacles and slowly your message will spread throughout the world. Even the shepherds are following the little sheep and have spread your message of love and peace to other parts of the country. You are especially loved by my Father and by myself as well. He has entrusted you with a love that is rare and has called you to set fire upon the earth. You must treasure that love and keep that fire alive in your hearts."

As Joshua said those words he crossed his arms on his breast, and in an instant his face became distorted with pain. Blood gushed from his hands, and he began to fall backward against the wall.

A little girl saw what happened and jumped to her feet and screamed. Another shot struck her in the head. She fell to the ground, lifeless. The marksman saw through the telescope what had happened, saw the girl fall to the ground, and was overcome with grief. It was his own daughter.

With his last bit of strength, Joshua fell to his knees, saw the girl lying there in a pool of blood, stretched out his bloody hand, and touched her. The gaping wound immediately healed. The girl opened her eyes, dazed, looked at Joshua, and smiled.

He smiled at her and fell to the ground.

The children panicked and screamed, not knowing what to do. The strangers sent to foil the plot, realizing what had happened and that they were too late, left immediately. Villagers came from all directions, rushing into the square. Women cried, looking frantically for their children. As men stood around the body of Joshua someone ran for the clergy. In no time Russ and Elmer were there, kneeling beside the body of the saintly stranger they had come to love. Elmer, who was always so controlled, burst into tears, crying, "Joshua, Joshua, our beloved friend, who was so gentle he could not harm even a broken flower! How could they do this? How could they?" The two men prayed over him, asking God "to bring him safely home far from this world of hatred and meanness. He was too good to live in our midst."

The doctor came, turned over the body, and, opening the shirt, examined Joshua. When the children saw the wounds in the heart and the wounds in the hands, one of them yelled out, "Look, it was God. It was Jesus. They killed God all over again and he was our friend. See what their hatred has done."

The children wept uncontrollably. When they saw Joshua heal the girl they all knew finally who Joshua really was, and everything he had said the past few days was now beginning to make sense, though they were too overwhelmed with grief to think about it.

The doctor asked some of the men to carry the body to the funeral director's house, but the older boys insisted on doing it, so the doctor let them. They reverently picked up the dead body of their friend and carried it across the square and down the street.

In no time reporters converged on the village, asking questions of everyone—clergy, bartenders, parents, children, Charlie the blacksmith, everyone who had anything to do with Joshua. Loaded with information, they went back to their offices to prepare their stories for the evening news and the next editions of the paper.

Elmer and Russ went to visit the other clergy and told them what had happened and suggested they all work together on a burial service for Joshua. They all agreed to do whatever they could. Since no church was large enough for everyone to fit, they decided to have the service in the ruins of an old monastery chapel outside the village, off in the meadow. It was a beautiful old building, even though part of the roof was gone and it was not clean. When word spread where the funeral was to be held, the whole town turned out to clean up the building and ready it for the occasion.

The funeral director cleaned the body of Joshua. It was decided he should be buried in his own clothes. Marie, Father Donnelly's housekeeper, took his clothes and washed them, so they would at least look clean.

It was decided that they would have the burial the very next day. It was Saturday. So deeply had he touched their lives that the whole village mourned that night like they had never grieved before, and they had not even known this man just a few months before. None of the children slept that night. Even crying all night didn't relieve their grief and the pain they felt over the loss of their friend who had taught them to love and to forgive. They prayed that God would forgive the ones who killed him.

CHAPTER 36

THE NEXT MORNING the whole village gathered at the funeral director's house and waited for the clergy. Having heard the news on the radio and seeing it on the television, children and adults came from faraway places for the funeral. Television crews came; reporters were everywhere.

When the clergy arrived the procession started. Teenagers acted as pallbearers, carrying the open coffin of their friend, every now and then looking down with tear-filled eyes at the body lying so peacefully in the coffin. John, the boy who played the drum on the march to the city, played muffled drumrolls through the village and across the meadow. It was mournful and heartrending as the procession meandered along the path through the meadow to the old church.

At the church the procession stopped, and the people stepped aside for the pallbearers and the clergy to pass through. Russ said the entrance prayers at the door to the church. Inside the church, the clergy together conducted a simple, dignified, but emotionally powerful service. Elmer had been asked to give the homily. It was brief but to the point, the kernel of which went as follows: "God sent into our midst a beautiful gift, a gift so precious that only innocent children were able to appreciate his value and draw him to their hearts. In the brief time he was among us the lives of our children changed forever, and not only their lives, but the lives of all of us as well. By the simple goodness of his life he taught us the beauty of values we preached but never experienced. Our village will never be the same. By showing a caring and accepting love for all of us, this simple stranger—only God knows who he really was—has taught us in a powerful way the basic truth of all religion—that we are all the children of God, belonging to the one family that he created. If we are to please him, we must begin from this day, never again to look upon our neighbors as strangers or as enemies but as one family. There can never again be divisions among us if we are to live in a way that is pleasing to God. This lesson has been burned into our hearts over the past few months by this good and gentle man. It is, I suppose, inevitable that the presence of goodness itself will never be allowed to exist in our midst except for a brief moment, until evil men, stung by the searing indictment of their own meanness, must rid themselves of a presence they cannot tolerate. It was true the first time, and it is no less true now. We do, however, have the beautiful memories of the goodness of Joshua forever branded on our minds and on our hearts, and the personal love he has shown for each one of us. There was no person who met him who did not become aware that they were totally and unconditionally loved by God, no matter what their faults or peculiarities or, yes, even their sins. We have all been blessed by God in his presence, and out of gratitude we cannot let his martyrdom pass in vain. We must carry on the message of his life until the love that he has shown us is spread far from the ruins of this decaying church into a new world that will share God's own vision of humanity as one family, all trying to understand their Father in their own limited and feeble way. And in ending all we can say is . . . 'Good-bye, dear friend. You have touched our lives forever.' "

By the time the priest finished there wasn't a dry eye in the church. Indeed, everyone's heart was breaking with grief. The words expressed in the homily were exactly what everyone was feeling, and it showed in the outpouring of tears, even those of strong men who had never cried before.

The Eucharist that morning was the most meaningful of their whole lives. He had been with them each day, without their realizing who he really was, and now all of them, regardless of denomination, were uniquely one in this sublime Presence that expressed so beautifully their new oneness in life.

All during the service the guitarists, the singers, the boy Joe taught to play the trumpet provided the music, playing things they had played so many times before. At one point they all played the pipes Joshua had given them the day of the march. At the end Joe and his friend played taps. While Joe played from inside the church the other boy was stationed out in the field and played the echo of each phrase, until the last note trailed off in the distance. It was heartrending and people cried uncontrollably.

After the service the clergy led the people in silent procession past the coffin for one last view of the body to pay their final respects. As each one passed, looking sadly into the crude wooden box, the reaction was the same, from the clergy to the children. Their faces became ashen, their look one of shock and then joy. The coffin was empty.

Outside the church the children gathered and started talking. "You see," one of them said, "it *was* Jesus. He even rose from the dead again."

Another added, "Yes, and he was our friend. He came to teach us a message and show us how to love, and they killed him."

"But what he taught us won't die," Peter said.

"That's true, and we have to make sure his message is carried out," one of the girls mentioned.

"What do you think we should do?" an older boy asked, half thinking out loud.

"I got an idea," said a boy whose father had been a close friend of the radical priest.

"What's that?" another asked.

"There are some who resisted right to this day and didn't even come to the church. Some are Catholics, some are Protestants. Why don't we get together and exchange parents?"

"How are we going to do that?" a girl asked.

"Just sit on each other's doorsteps until they take us in," answered the boy who made the suggestion.

Some didn't think it was a good idea, but the kids whose parents were resistant, and may have even been part of the plot, wanted to do something heroic to atone for what their parents had done. They thought it was a great idea and decided to do it.

"Suppose they don't take us in?" one girl questioned.

"We'll just sit there until they do, even if we have to starve. They will eventually be shamed in front of the rest of the town if they don't take us in. Then, when they change their attitudes, we'll go back home."

The kids didn't realize it, but reporters were standing behind them all during the exchange, jotting down everything the kids said. It would be in every newspaper in the country before the day was out, creating tremendous pressure on the recalcitrant parents. As it turned out the marksman, whose bullet struck his own daughter and whom Joshua healed, was so conscience stricken after seeing Joshua touch and heal her, he became the kids' best ally, telling all his cronies secretly what had happened. With his help, the kids' strategy would work.

When the little girl had gone home on that Friday afternoon, her father was not there. During the commotion in the square he slipped out to the meadow and buried the rifle deep in the ground. He sat in the field and cried like a baby, overwhelmed by the terrible evil he had done.

His eyes were bloodshot and his face had a tortured look when he arrived at his house and walked into the kitchen. The family, together with a houseful of neighbors, was all astir, excitedly questioning the girl about what happened in the square. She didn't remember very much. Her father was silent and passed unnoticed in the confusion. He looked at his daughter, closely scrutinizing the side of her head where the bullet struck. There was not the slightest trace of a wound. He couldn't even let her know what had happened. He simply stood around, dumb and outwardly emotionless. He was usually considered odd anyway, so no one thought his behavior any stranger than usual.

At Joshua's funeral the girl's father had sat with his whole family. At times during the service he cried uncontrollably, which made his family wonder; previously, he had shown nothing but anger and suspicion over the work the stranger carried on with the children.

After the funeral, he went off with his cronies and told them all that had happened. They could see how broken up he was over what he had done and were afraid he might betray them all in his grief. He told them they had nothing to fear, but still managed to shake their consciences. Reluctantly, they went along when he insisted that they cooperate with the children's plan to exchange parents. They were more afraid of what he might do if they didn't go along with them.

Children all across the country, fired up by the news stories and the television coverage, were more determined than ever to carry on the message of this simple man whose coming was so unobtrusive and whose presence was so brief, but whose extraordinary love and caring changed the lives of all who accepted him.

John Hourihan's ecumenical school became more popular than ever, forcing its board to initiate double class sessions to accommodate the increased enrollment.

The two bishops who authored the pastoral letter gave sermons on Joshua that Sunday. They held a joint service in the Anglican cathedral honoring Joshua and his work, and encouraged people not to fear drawing closer to one another in a unity that could only be pleasing to God.

But most remarkable of all was that almost overnight the children throughout the land came to dominate the political life of the country, and they did it in the spirit and gentle ways of Joshua. Politicians and activists were

shamed into cooperating with the programs and suggestions advocated by the young people, whose influence in
society was universal and profound.

A new day had dawned, a new spirit spread throughout
the land, and it all seemed to have happened because of the
simple, unassuming goodness of one gentle stranger who
knew only how to love.